C000213977

How To Build a Fortune

by Thomas Tapper, Litt. D.

with an introduction by Roger Chambers

This work contains material that was originally published in 1913.

This publication was created and published for the public benefit, utilizing public funding and is within the Public Domain.

This edition is reprinted for educational purposes and in accordance with all applicable Federal Laws.

Introduction Copyright 2018 by Roger Chambers

COVER CREDITS

Front Cover -
Gold bullion ap 001 by *Slav4*|Ariel Palmon
[CC BY-SA 3.0 - https://creativecommons.org/licenses/by-sa/3.0]
via Wikimedia Commons

Back Cover -
US Dollars One Hundred Banknotes by Milad Mosapoor
[Public Domain]
via Wikimedia Commons

Quote -
From the back cover and interior :
"Every man is the Architect of his own fortune."
Atributed to Appius Claudius Caecus (Roman Censor)
via Oxford Reference [OxfordReference.com]

PLEASE NOTE :

As with all reprinted books of this age that are intended to perfectly reproduce the original edition, considerable pains and effort had to be undertaken to correct fading and sometimes outright damage to existing proofs of this title. At times, this task can be quite monumental, requiring an almost total rebuilding of some pages from digital proofs of multiple copies. Despite this, imperfections still sometimes exist in the final proof and may detract slightly from the visual appearance of the text.

DISCLAIMER :

Due to the age of this book, some methods or practices may have been deemed unsafe or unacceptable in the interim years. In utilizing the information herein, you do so at your own risk. We republish antiquarian books without judgment or revisionism, solely for their historical and cultural importance, and for educational purposes.

Self Reliance Books

Get more historic titles on animal and stock breeding, gardening and old fashioned skills by visiting us at:

http://selfreliancebooks.blogspot.com/

~ introduction ~

Here at **Self-Reliance Books** we are dedicated to bringing you the best in *dusty-old-book-knowledge* to help you in your quest for self-sufficiency and food independence. But here's one that's a little bit of a departure, but still in a similar realm – ***How to Build a Fortune***.

It was written by Thomas Tapper, Litt. D., and first published in 1913, making it over one-hundred years old.

This antiquarian text features chapters on *Making a Beginning, The Earning Capacity, Appropriation, Getting Rich in a Hurry, The Value of Money*, and *Little Philanthropies*, plus more.

Tapper received a *Litterarum* doctorate (*Doctor of Letters*,) and made his mark as a composer, musician, lecturer, writer and editor. He is best known for his work *Lives of Great Composers*, a picture-book series.

This old book is a must-have for all enthusiasts of wealth and finance how-to books, and all those interested in the subject in the historical aspect.

~ Roger Chambers

State of Jefferson, April 2019

TO

John T. Windrim, Esq.

Every man is the Architect of his own fortune

PREFACE

The purpose of this little book is to point out that when thought and skill are expended in earning money, the money itself is worthy of as much respect as the thought and skill that produced it.

Men and women who work for a limited income, arrive one day at the threshold of old age. They should not cross this threshold empty-handed. They should have with them sufficient of the fruits of their years of labor to protect the last days.

Want and misery need not be the portion of anyone who will work. It only requires that one labor earnestly, and spend prudently, to be assured of a protecting margin.

As this text is addressed to humble workers rather than to people of plentiful means, nothing is said in these chapters to encourage speculation in any form. Emphasis is laid upon the necessity and reliability of savings banks, life insurance, and of conservative bonds in small denominations. The family that possesses a home, and has saved something in one or more of these three channels, is enviably situated.

Old age protection, however, is not to be thought of entirely from the standpoint of money.

In the years that one labors and saves it is equally essential that one shall study and meditate upon those things which, in their turn, result in a mental enrichment. These are no less a comfort and protection in the last years than is money itself.

It is in the hope of stimulating young Americans to the attainment of both these forms of wealth: wealth of Earning Power and wealth of Learning Power, that this little book has been written.

New York, October 4, 1913.

CONTENTS

6

HOW TO BUILD A FORTUNE

HOW TO BUILD A FORTUNE

CHAPTER I

MAKING A BEGINNING

Turn idle wishes into energetic action and the thing is accomplished.

We begin to build a fortune, not with money but with thought.

It has been said many times that it is far easier to earn money than it is to save it. This statement is true, and the truth of it should suggest the fact that as a man earns only by the application of thought and labor, so he saves only by the same application. Saving is a process carefully to be considered, studied, and put into working order. Any man who has given the problem the thought it deserves will have discovered two facts:

(1) All saving results from spending less than one earns.

(2) The potentiality of money saved to-day depends entirely on the manner in which it is laid out in order that it may earn more money in the future. In other words, we must be ever mindful of Benjamin Franklin's famous dictum:

"Money earns money; but the money, money makes, earns more money."

Every man, intent on saving for the future, must take unto himself indispensable partners. They are Industry, Perseverance, and Time.

INDUSTRY insures the creation and perpetuation of the general earning fund from which savings are made.

PERSEVERANCE insures the continuous operation, the onward motion of the saving plan.

TIME is the factor that permits money to

develop and to increase its interest earning power.

Who can save?

Everyone who earns.

This may not seem, at first sight, to be so. But the truth of it has been demonstrated so often that we should no longer doubt it. The amount saved from time to time may be small, but when small savings are brought under the influence of Perseverance and Time, they become significant. The story is told of a New Hampshire farmer who set aside every day for fifty years, a five-cent piece, depositing each dollar as he accumulated it, in a savings bank. He began to do this at eighteen. At sixty-eight, he has to his credit, two thousand, nine hundred dollars—a sum that earns annually, at five per cent, one hundred and forty-five dollars, or eight times the annual amount he deposited.

The average earner of money, whether the annual income be large or small, must resolve that some of the so-called pleasures that may be bought with money to-day, be given up, in order that their cost may be set aside to buy necessities in the future when the working capacity has been reduced by the passing years. Few are willing to do this. The desire to possess Now everything that money will buy, whether it be needed or not, is the one great cause of old-age poverty.

Even the man who is entirely free of responsibility toward others must take into account the fact of his responsibility to his own future. A man whose wages are as low as ten dollars a week, or five hundred and twenty dollars a year, would require to invest at five per cent, a fund of ten thousand, four hundred dollars to assure himself of the same income in old age. Thus:

Principal, safely invested.............. $10,400
At five per cent.................... .05
_____
Annual income $520.00

A family, the head of which earns ten thousand dollars a year, would require in the event of his death the income at five per cent on a fund of two hundred thousand dollars, to continue to live as they had. This shows that working power has a capitalization value far above what we realize. It is on this value that a man should base all his calculations of expenditure and saving. He may never accumulate the full amount of his capitalized value, but he must accumulate something that will supplement his lessening earning power as the years leave their impress upon him.

Let us take the case of the man who has no responsibilities beyond himself, in order to ascertain how he, as a type of all others, must proceed to begin the preliminary study of saving. How shall he adjust himself toward money so that he may learn to make a logical apportionment of his income?

If he holds that he must not live on the bounty of others, but by his own exertions, he will find that he must count on four fundamental expenses, *not three,* as is usually the case.

They are these:

1. A place to sleep where the body will be safe.
2. Sufficient clothing.
3. Nourishing food.
4. Toll,* paid out of his earnings for future protection.

The first three are secured, in some degree, by nearly all people, for they are the fundamental protection of life itself. Of those that secure shelter, food and clothing by their own labor, an amazing number never think of the fourth, or future protection, but are willing to exchange it, on the spot, for one or many of the inessential things that may happen to strike the fancy at the moment. In this connection it has been said that if young men would deposit pennies in the savings bank with the unfailing regularity that they pass over nickels, dimes, and quarters to the keep-

---

*Toll: The original meaning of this word was "that which is counted out in payment."

ers of saloons, cigar stands, and the like, they would never need fear an unprotected old age.

The first step then is APPROPRIATION.

The first item to put down on paper is not only the amount of wages received annually, but the factors that are active in earning the wages.

A typical case may be illustrated thus:

```
Annual income ..................... $1,000
Earned by
            Knowledge
            Skill
            Health
            Reliability
            _____
Value.......... $1,000
```

Should it be desired to earn more money, *both* factors must be increased. Thus:

```
Annual income..............more than $1,000
To be earned by
                Knowledge
                Skill
                Health
                Reliability
                Ambition
                Study
                _____
Value......more than $1,000
```

We will return to these factors later. Out of the total annual income there must be taken at once the cost of shelter, food, and clothing. If the subtraction shows that these three items demand more than the annual income, or all of it, one of two things must happen: either more money must be earned or less money must be spent. At first either alternative seems as hard as the other. The wise thing to do then is to make a re-apportionment and bring, by strictest economy (which, by the way, means administration), the annual expenditure below the annual income. It can be done, and, further than that, a wise person will see that it is done.

There is now a margin in hand. May not one do with it what one wishes? Logically, no. There is still a fourth fundamental expense to pay for regularly; namely, future protection. One may or may not be inclined to put all surplus aside to a future fund; but he may be assured that what he deposits in the savings bank, or pays out for life insurance, or otherwise invests, he will have; and

what he puts into soda, cigars, and hard
drinks, he will not have. Here is where each
one of us makes his own decision and with
the decision come the consequences.

Let us look at it in this way:

Assume the annual income at thirty is.. $800.00
Total necessary expenses 700.00
_____
Balance $100.00

Further, let us assume that this program
will be carried on for twenty-five years.

Two results are possible, by two opposite
methods.

Method No. 1 : *Waste the money.* Waste,
like all other acts, has its consequences. If
the money be simply spent thoughtlessly, the
spender is accumulating a thoughtless system
of action for twenty-five years. This will affect not only the amount of money involved
in this operation, but it will gradually creep
into all his affairs. On the other hand, this
money may not be simply wasted thoughtlessly, but it may be spent, let us say, for
drink. In this instance, he has devoted

twenty-five years to undermining his health and lessening his capacity from thirty to fifty-five, and from fifty-five to the end of his life.

Method No. 2. *Save the money.* By this method, there will be credited the principal and compound interest on one hundred dollars, set aside annually for twenty-five years. The total principal will amount to $2,500 and the accumulated interest to $1,831.20, which makes a total of $4,331.20, providing a gross principal that will yield annually, at five per cent, $216.56, and this not only during the lifetime of the investor, but forever, if he so cares to devise it.

Saving, to be a success, must necessarily be practiced for a definite purpose. The mere accumulation of money is not a worthy inspiration. The use of money, we must remember, is strictly confined to the present life. And to this life we must look for the saving's object.

It may be to build a home, to educate children, to furnish protection in old age; whatever it is, the object should be worth while and not based on the love of money itself.

The young man may marry, and in that event he finds all the incentive to save that anyone need have. When the wedding day comes he should have enough cash in hand to begin the business (which it is) of family home life; and, further, he should have enough life insurance to protect the girl who has entrusted her life and loyalty to him.

And this is no great act to be looked upon as a sacrifice. It is the ordinary fair-play that one owes to another.

Then it pays to think ahead. Human strength is bound to grow less some day, and, after that, to keep on growing less. A man may be well along in life before this happens, but it should not find him unprepared. He ought to think of this and begin in youth to prepare for it.

A good many tell us that we need not worry. "You will get along somehow." Don't believe it. "Somehow" may have promises in its pockets, but it supplies no wants. We have to do that.

Let no one despise the day of small things. If you can put away only a twenty-five cent piece now and then, do it. Four of them make one dollar, and that amount earns interest in the savings bank.

The hard part of the savings habit is keeping it going. We can begin it with as much confidence as the man who boasts that he can "quit smoking when he wants to." It takes two to do that: the Man and the Habit. And the habit throws the man a good many times before he finally gets it down.

The first step toward saving is to start. That is easy. After the first step is taken the fight begins. But if you have an object you will win out, if you remember that every step brings you nearer to it.

But let us not love money save for the best purposes it can accomplish. Readers of Balzac's great book, *Eugenie Grandet,* will remember the inordinate passion for money that Grandet possessed. He loved the sight and the touch of it. When his wife lay dying, all he could think to offer her was the privilege of seeing the golden coins run through his fingers as he dropped them on the bed. Grandet's pursuit of money was not inspired by economy, but by avarice.

Samuel Johnson, the English author and lexicographer, once met Richard Savage on a day when he had received his small annual allowance. At that time scarlet coats were in fashion, and Savage had spent all his money to provide himself with one, though his toes were sticking out of his shoes at the time. Savage was absolutely incapable of judging the present and future value of money.

The man intent on building a fortune *and of enjoying life every day of life,* will choose between these two extremes and avoid the terrible catastrophe that awaits him.

Money is not to be regarded as a gift of the gods, or as a pleasant contribution from Good Luck. When a man earns money he gives of his very self for it. It comes as the reward for labor of some kind—either labor of muscle, or of mind, or both. To waste money, then, is to waste strength of muscle and of mind, a point of view that should throw the inadvisability of the act into bolder relief.

To have skill and strength for service, to receive for them a fair equivalent in money, to apportion that money so that wants and desires lie within it, and to carry a portion of it forward for future use, when skill and strength have a lessened market value, these steps constitute the beginning of all fortune building, however simple or extensive.

CHAPTER II

THE EARNING CAPACITY

"If you want to know whether you are destined to be a success or a failure in life you can easily find out. The test is simple and it is infallible: ARE YOU ABLE TO SAVE MONEY? If not, drop out. You will lose. You may think not, but you will lose as sure as you live. The seed of success is not in you."—JAMES J. HILL.

We referred, in the preceding chapter, to the factors that are active in the earning of money. They are more numerous than we usually suppose. To begin with, work, even of the humblest sort, requires some degree of skill. Street-sweeping may be done well or ill and no more may be said of the work that falls to the hands of the most important man of affairs.

Skill is a quality, not of muscle but of mind. Every worker must strive to master his work with the mind until his mastery of it is complete. When he has reached that point, he is invariably ready for better work, and he as invariably finds it.

In order that mind and body may be devoted to work as they should be, the worker must possess health. Health is the condition that permits one to do work with a clear perception of what it calls for, and sufficient strength to meet its demands.

Just as it is necessary to attain skill, so it is necessary to maintain health. Hence, a wise man will forego the inessential pleasures that interfere with the free expression of himself as a worker. He will accustom himself to simple food that gives the maximum of nourishment; things, however tempting in appearance, he will avoid if they unfit him for his best efforts; he will secure the necessary amount of sleep to bring body and mind in tune again. In brief, he will guard his health unceasingly, because it is his capital.

The third factor with which we work is Time. It not only provides us with the hours for work itself, but with other hours for rest and for the increase of skill. There is no portion of the day more valuable to the worker than his leisure. It means opportunity for culture, study, amusement, and many other possibilities equally essential. What men have done in their leisure hours to attain a greater degree of skill, has been told in many books. This use of leisure, yielding greater skill, ultimately results in increased earning ability; in fact, in greater fortune.

He is a wise worker who is forever active in mind, seeking a broader outlet for his capacity. The study hour is, in fact, investment. By study, the mind is not only enriched, but it gains power. It analyzes more closely, sees farther, comprehends more quickly. Hence, more mind is the result. As every one works primarily with the mind, he will work more and better who is constantly increasing its power.

It has been said that most careers are made after supper. The fact is, all careers are made after supper: Some for good, some for ill, some for not much of anything. But whatever it is, it is shaped and fashioned after six o'clock.

And from this fact we can deduce this bit of wisdom:

A man is worth just about as much as he gets out of his leisure hours.

What have we before us when the day's work is done? Four or five hours of the best part of the day. If one is ambitious, here is the great opportunity to study out the one plan that should interest everybody, namely:

What should I strive to be, to do, and to have?

The story is interesting of a man who set to work to discover how he could earn more money. His position paid him well for what he had to do. But to do it, required of him this daily program:

> 5.30   Arise and prepare for breakfast.
> 6.30   Walk to the train.
> 6.30-8.30 Spent reaching the office.
> 8.45-12   Office work.
> 12-1   Lunch.

1-5   Office work.
5-7   Travel home.
7-8   Dinner.
8-9.30   Rest from the day's work.

Here is a program that renders life arduous simply because of the geographical relation between home and office. The man in question moved into town and took a room near his place of business—with this result:

7   Arise and prepare for breakfast.
7.30-8   Breakfast.
8-8.30   Writing (for details see below).
8.30-8.45 To office.
8.45-5   As before.
5-6.30   Home and dinner.
6.30-10.30 or later—Writing.

Now the result of this in writing has been a number of articles for the newspapers and four books, all of which will earn him a royalty income for years. Incidentally it may be pointed out that this man is a far better office worker than ever before, because he is doing two kinds of work instead of one; with the result that there is no monotony in his day. Furthermore, instead of working from day to day, he now has a "long plan." His literary work is shaping an activity for the future that is, in itself, an inspiration.

Each one of us must shape his own course. Life is not paddling a canoe in a mill pond. It is the mastery of a ship that sails far out to sea.

Included in the factors of the earning capacity is this art of the long plan. We must not drift, nor decide on a short trip, but prepare for a journey worth while.

The principal factors, then, that are operative in work, are skill, health and the use of leisure. Many others might be included but these are the all-embracing essentials and include industry, perseverance, honest endeavor, the fulfillment of responsibility and the like. They include, also, that one great factor that is fundamental to all labor for and with others, reliability; the quality that stimulates trust and creates a basis for faith.

Back of these factors, and required by the

pursuit of them, is another that is fundamental to all fortune building. This is self-
denial. From the practice of self-denial we
learn a lesson that is valuable in the effort to
save money. This lesson teaches us that we
can spend Thought and Time in precisely the
way we spend money; either wantonly, or for
value received; for the needs and pleasures of
the moment alone, or for these and for the
needs, pleasures and protection of the future
as well.

When we begin to build a fortune, we too
often forget that we must lay up not only
money but those things that are uncorruptible
by moth and rust. The future must be pro-
tected not alone by financial resources but by
mental resources as well. The increase of
skill is a perpetual increase in the joy of work.
Health guarded in early years is in itself an
insurance for old age. The wise use of leisure
enriches the mind, multiplies one's interests
in life, and provides, as well as it is humanly
possible to provide, against affliction.

The fortune builder must not fail to build

with these bricks as well as with money. He must, early in life, be convinced of their actual importance to him in later years. But while he is busily engaged in fortune building for the future, he must not overlook the fact that he is alive To-day; he is living Now, in the present, and he must live it fully and happily, letting each day pay to him its toll of skill attained, of pleasure secured in labor and leisure, and of satisfaction in what it stores up for the days to come.

Grandet saved for the future, but his avarice day by day destroyed that future as it came to him. Conversely, the spendthrift does not live for to-day in his pursuit of pleasure; he consumes to-morrow with it. Each is unwise in his day and generation.

Men who have faced the world fearlessly have invariably won success by following an actual plan. They have created something in thought that they have worked out in deed. They saw the truth and proved it a fact by making it an act. Hence, we have various sets of rules for conduct, precepts for those who may want to go and do likewise. As a matter of fact, however, every man must make his own rules. They must grow out of his experience and fit perfectly his mental picture of what he wants to be.

And yet such rules, particularly from men who have made good, are always interesting.

When Meyer Rothschild, founder of the great banking house in Frankfort, Germany, died, he left something better than wealth; an example that has become a tradition in this noted family. He also left precepts. Among them were the following:

Carefully examine every detail of your business.

Be prompt in everything.

Take time to consider, but decide positively.

Dare to go forward.

Bear troubles patiently.

Be brave in the struggle of life.

Maintain your integrity as a sacred thing.

Never tell business lies.

Make no useless acquaintances.

Pay your debts promptly.

Shun strong liquors.

Employ your time well.

Do not reckon on chance.

Work hard.

John Donough, whose name is as familiar to every child of New Orleans as that of Washington, attributed to the conduct which resulted from the following precepts, all his success in life: In fact, so much did he value them that he ordered them cut on his tombstone.

Remember that labor is one of the conditions of existence.

Time is gold; throw not one minute away, but place each to account.

Do unto all men as you would be done by.

Never put off till to-morrow what can be done to-day.

Never bid another do what you can do for yourself.

Never covet what is not your own.

Never think any matter so trifling as not to deserve notice.

Never give out what does not come in.

Do not spend, but produce.

Let the greatest order regulate the actions of your life.

Study in your course of life to do the greatest amount of good.

Deprive yourself of nothing that is necessary to your comfort, but live in honorable simplicity and frugality.

Labor, then, to the last moment of your existence.

Many men of to-day have given sterling advice to young men and women as to how to improve their working equipment. To W. L. Park, Vice-President and General Manager of the Illinois Central Railroad, is attributed the excellent advice, *to cultivate the study habit.* Commenting upon this, the Chicago *Record-Herald* said:

"This is good advice, not only for railroad men, but for every worker. The man who studies constantly the principles that apply to his work will produce better results than the man who goes along doing things as he has been taught to do them, and he will also progress mentally. If, further, he studies how other workers in his line do things, he will become an expert.

"There is a belief among the uneducated that education is a magic acquisition, obtained for a lifetime by a college or technical school course. But the habit of study throughout life marks the progressive from the unprogressive worker, whatever the educational start.

"The educational bureau of the Illinois Central is intended to aid by study men who do things. Such a bureau might well be created by every corporation. Study combined with practical work is the order of the newer technical education. It has produced admirable results in Germany, and is coming rapidly into favor in the United States."

Another railway company, the Rock Island, issued a bulletin to its employés asking each one of them "to incorporate himself at a capital in accordance with his salary, and make himself as valuable as other investments represented by an equal capital.

"Say you earn one thousand dollars a year," says the bulletin. "At four per cent, that is the yearly interest on twenty-five thousand dollars. In other words, the company capitalizes you at twenty-five thousand dollars, and willingly pays interest on that sum for the use of your energy and faculties.

"You are thus capitalized for just about what a modern locomotive costs. You may not have as much pull, but you ought to have as much push. Remember that the locomotive can't add figures, nor run a typewriter, nor select and compile statistics.

"You can last a lot longer and run a great deal further than the best engine ever built.

"Most of all, you can make yourself constantly worth more, while the locomotive is never worth a cent more than it was the day it was built.

"It rests with you. Make your twenty-five thousand dollar valuation climb to fifty thousand dollars, to one hundred thousand dollars, to five hundred thousand dollars. Select your food with care. Treat decently the body on which your mind depends for its strength and sanity.

"Above all, feed your mind. Read, study, and observe. Like the engine, you can't do your work unless you stay on the rails and keep where the boss can find you.

"Just remember that no call-boy ever found an engine in a saloon dive, or other place of that sort."

The factors, then, that earn money, are superior to money itself. Indeed, a skillful man who has guarded his health, and has a proper perception of the use and value of time, is richer than money can make him. He is capable, at almost any period in life, of insuring himself against misfortune; in fact he may consider himself wealthy, not in great possessions, but in the skill with which he can maintain himself in the working world.

Youth is preëminently the storing-up time of life. It is then, if ever, that the essential pleasures of life may be learned and accepted as a permanent possession. With them, life is a richer possibility to the end; without them, it is a catastrophe.   A man is limited in the extent to which he can shelter, feed, and clothe himself; but he need not be limited, except by his own choice, in the treasures of art, of books, of friendship, of ambition, of all the possessions, in fact, that are beyond price.

The blessings of poverty have been over-sung, but the pleasures of life that are possible without great wealth have never been exaggerated.

CHAPTER III

APPROPRIATION

He has become a wise man who has learned to govern his own money.

The lessons to be learned before one can begin to build a fortune are essential to all grades of people, from the humble in possession to the very wealthy. Those lowest in the scale must master the elementary principles of management and emerge as rapidly as they can from a purposeless method of existence into one that is marked by some degree, at least, of self-government and careful administration. Those higher in the scale of wealth are as unfortunate in a sense as those who have no wealth, if in their eagerness to be possessed of more and more money they fail to provide themselves with the means for procuring those numerous pleasures of life that are not to be purchased by money alone.

Money is a symbol. It stands for Value. The thing that creates money is Labor. This may be the labor of body which does manual work, or the labor of mind that plans great undertakings and involves the activities of many people.

To regard money as a symbol of labor, that is, to regard it *as labor in another form*, is to give it its proper place and to recognize in it its rightful dignity. No man, poor or rich, has any right to misunderstand this vital characteristic of money. He is not justified in debasing it or himself by wasting it; nor is he justified in dealing with it, in his daily life, save as a good steward.

Now, a good steward is a good administrator. He fixes in mind as a perfect equation, this:

To think *equals* To do.

To do *equals* To have.

This principle has played an important part in the economy of nations. It is said that on the oldest bank notes of the world, issued by the Chinese treasury, there appeared the name of the bank, date of issue, denomination, number, signature, and the picture of a heap of coins which totaled the value of the note. This last device, if it appeared on a one dollar bill, would show a picture of ten dimes or any combination of coins equal to one dollar.

But these old bank notes of China bore a legend that we have not yet mastered to the full. It was this:

"PRODUCE ALL YOU CAN. SPEND WITH ECONOMY."

What other combination of so few words so forcibly states the whole subject of national and individual economies?

We have only to turn the light of the negative on these two sentences to see that prosperity for anyone is purely an individual matter.

PRODUCE ALL YOU CAN means:

Do not loaf. Do not sponge, borrow, beg or steal. Do not live on the efforts of somebody else. Do not consume without return. Do not fail to give for what you expect to get.

And SPEND WITH ECONOMY suggests to us:

Do not waste. Do not buy uselessly. Do not buy foolishly. Do not desire what you can get along without. Do not think what good times you can have if the grocery bill is still unreceipted.

We know a great deal in these happy times. But we do not know everything. We do not know even a remnant of the ancient wisdom that made prosperous nations centuries before Columbus played as a boy with his little toy boats.

Suppose we should try this legend of the Chinese for one week, and work for six days, producing the best there is in us; then account, on the basis of actual reason and economy, for every penny we spend. One would be a new individual.

Hence, the fundamental principles are:

(1) To know the value and importance of money.

(2) To account honestly and accurately for all one receives and expends.

This is appropriation.

Appropriation is the just distribution of money as dictated by the necessities of life. When the necessities of life (never omitting future protection as a fundamental item) have been paid for, we may begin to think of the luxuries, but not before. Even then, we should think twice about them before they ride over us, and seem to become, in their turn, necessities.

You earn a certain sum of money per annum. Write down the amount. You have certain absolutely necessary expenses. Write down each of them. Perhaps you have never kept an account so that you have an exact knowledge of your daily expenditures for these necessities. And it is quite as unlikely that you know accurately what other items of expense you have created that in the course of a year exhaust your resources.

Write down next the statement that you will forever cease to live this scrambled sort of financial life. And, furthermore, that you will henceforth avoid confusing the necessities of life with the dictates of your habits.

It is now required to determine what the necessities of your life are, and what they may cost on the basis of your income. To determine this is to take the initial step in learning the art of appropriation.

At this point, explicit rules, in the pages of a book, applicable alike for all people, are impossible. Every human being is surrounded by conditions peculiarly his own. They must be recognized and reckoned with; they must be made the point of departure. Rules that should logically govern a married man, with a family, receiving a moderate income, do not apply to a single man earning the same income. This brings before us the question of the extent of responsibility. But, reverting to the statement of necessities in the first chapter, it is true for both of them that they must be sheltered, clothed, fed, and that they must, in one way or another, pay regularly for future protection.

It has been generally accepted, as a safe rule to follow, that not more than from one-fourth to one-fifth of a man's income should be paid for rent. This has been expressed in another way: A week's income should pay a month's rent. The amount necessary to appropriate for food and clothing must depend on the number of people in the family who are dependent on the wage earner. It must be left to good judgment and good management that these two items be kept within reasonable limits.

What are reasonable limits?

To answer this question brings us face to face with the entire question of household administration. If a man earns two dollars per day it is obvious that the family can save considerable money by not spending it unwisely. The domestic administration requires that the husband or wife attend personally to the marketing, buying wholesome food as economically as possible. It is the duty of the wife to know how to make this food go as far as possible, to prepare it in a wholesome and appetizing manner, and to master the one fundamental lesson of wasting nothing. This throws the art of building a fortune back upon the skill in family management. It shows that a fortune does not come alone from saving money but from an economy applied to spending for everything that costs money.

It is said that the French "have no garbage pails," a statement in which there is contained a great sermon on the modern extravagance of those whose garbage pails, of one kind or another, are always full.

The next necessity, clothing, is to be treated in the same way. A working man and a working man's family can be clothed with the same care they can be fed, and they can be clothed so that tailors' bills are few and never a menace to the safety of the family income.

Here, again, household administration must solve the problem as an economic question.

Formerly, the family clothing was the handiwork of the wife. The custom is so fast disappearing that we find little trace of it now. It is the universal desire, nowadays, to purchase clothing from makers who offer well-cut and stylish garments. It is seldom purchased for its wearing qualities, but primarily for its appearance. If this way of procuring clothing is necessary, the family economy must at least find some basis for action in the effort to learn the care of clothing, for good care is a guarantee of a longer lease of life and usefulness.

These observations, simple as they are, show us that the main question, after all, is attitude towards necessities. If one learns gradually skillful administration, which is but another name for common sense applied to daily life, it will be found that even a little money can be made to go a long way. Conversely, if family life proceeds without care or forethought, no amount of money will ever be sufficient to keep up with its habits of carelessness.

Wise appropriation, then, rests on skillful management. It is skillful management alone that will make it possible for the pay envelope to meet all necessary demands and to leave, over and above them, something for the one particular item that the vast majority of people never think of; namely, the regularly set aside amount for future protection.

Anyone who has never given attention to the science of spending money, and who has never followed a definite system of personal and family administration, can form no adequate idea of the extent to which they influence finances. It is easier by far even for the unskilled to earn money than to care for it. Back of most family poverty lack of management is found more frequently than lack of income in wages. So long as an individual or a family follows the hand to mouth rule, just so long is any degree of well-being impossible. This shows us the truth of the opening line of the first chapter, which states that we begin to build a fortune not with money in the pocket, but with thought.

Every wage earner is, in a sense, in business. His skill, knowledge and strength are his stock in trade. His wages represent more or less justly the value of his stock in trade in the market. No wise business man would think of conducting his affairs without a permanent record day by day of its activity. The wage earner should take a hint from this practice and keep a detailed statement of all he receives and all he expends. Otherwise, it is impossible for him accurately to begin the practice of appropriation.

The subject of appropriation in household expenditure has been discussed by many writers. The following table has been widely published and may be taken as a type:

	Per cent
Rent (or interest on mortgage and taxes)	20
Table	25
Light and fuel	5
Clothing	10
Incidentals	5
Emergency (Physician's care, etc.)	5
Life insurance	15
General savings' account	10
Philanthropy (Church, charities, etc.)	5
Total	100

Applied to incomes of seven hundred and fifty dollars, a thousand dollars, and twelve hundred and fifty dollars per annum, or, fifteen dollars, twenty dollars, and twenty-five dollars per week, this appropriation plan gives the following:

	$750.00 a year	$1,000.00 a year	$1,250.00 a year
Rent	$150.00	$200.00	$250.00
Table	187.50	250.00	312.50
Light and fuel..	37.50	50.00	62.50
Clothing	75.00	100.00	125.00
Incidentals	37.50	50.00	62.50
Emergency	37.50	50.00	62.50
Life insurance ...	112.50	150.00	187.50
Savings	75.00	100.00	125.00
Philanthropy	37.50	50.00	62.50
Total	$750.00	$1,000.00	$1,250.00

Now, such tables can mean but one thing, and that one thing is System. Out of a hundred men, possibly not five earning a thousand dollars a year could be found to lay it out in exactly the manner shown above. That is not the essential fact. But this is: There must be some method back of all family finances or the family will be constantly without money.

There is no better way to fix upon a spending system than to join it to a savings system. One not only helps the other but each is indispensable to the other.

A writer * commenting on this principle, says:

"Fixed charges are seldom burdensome; it is the spasmodic, irregular, and unusual outlay that is felt with a sense of deprivation. Even the haphazard deposit of money in a savings bank costs an effort of the will. But a definite plan of expenditure that is thought out and arranged for in advance, as the disposal of a part of one's income in a beneficial way, is no more repellent or irksome than the payment of money for food, clothing or shelter."

And continuing, the same writer says:

"Experience of the race proves that the only way that one can 'get money' is by economy and by the saving of one's surplus, and it is equally true that the only effective way to save is to do it *systematically*.

———

* J. E. McLean, of the American Real Estate Company.

"To accomplish this, three conditions are essential:

"(1) The saving must be done regularly and methodically, according to a definite system.

"(2) The money must be deposited in a safe place.

"(3) It must be so invested as to yield a legitimate interest return to its owner.

"Human nature is so constituted that what we do regularly a few times becomes a habit, and what is habitual is always easy, whether it be a virtue or a vice. But the cultivation of the former, it would seem, calls for more or less self-discipline on the part of every one—even the best of us."

Chapter IV

KEEPING ACCOUNTS

Sail without a chart and you never know where the ship is taking you.

The preceding chapter should have made it clear that every man must devise his own system of appropriation, adapting it as closely as he can to his peculiar circumstances. And it should be no less clear that a necessary factor in every effort at appropriation is an accurate record of expenditure, covering a period long enough to show what the habits are that create expenses. This brings us to the subject of keeping accounts.

In our love for freedom we are inclined to think that all restriction is servitude. We immediately rebel against any systematic act that results in revealing us to ourselves. But true freedom is the child, not of carelessness but of forethought and just self-government.

No man can find true pleasure in life who refuses to care for the physical body. The very possession of the body makes it incumbent on us to seek freedom by first giving it the due amount of care that makes freedom possible. This is equally true of money. To possess whatever portion of freedom we can have through money, we must devote careful thought to it. Unwatched financial operations, however small, like the uncared for body, soon cause trouble.

What is the ultimate object of keeping accounts?

Primarily, it makes the humblest wage earner a good business man, in that it permits him to see at a glance what he takes in, what he gives out, and also, *what he receives for what he gives out.*

No elaborate form of bookkeeping is necessary to keep accounts accurately. The prime necessity is to ascertain where the money goes. Few men know that. When questioned, they forget the countless little things that have, in the course of time, established themselves as habits to be paid for. Get a pocket account book for a few cents, and devote some months, or a year, to recording the history of every penny. If you rebel at this practice it is probably because you are cowardly; you are afraid to see yourself in the mirror of your own financial transactions. Or, you may rebel at the trouble. But why a man who prides himself on Sunday on being made in the Divine image, should think it beneath his dignity to know what he has done with the money *for which he gives his thought and strength* on the other six days, is not clear.

It is worth while to dismiss this, and similar objections, and to get down to business. An accurate record of small and great expenses, day by day, for a year, is no child's play. It requires character to do it right, and it develops the character of one who does it. If you have a feeling of revulsion at seeing on paper in your own handwriting, the recurrence of five or ten cents every day for

beer, or ten, twenty, or thirty cents for cigars
or cigarettes, it is worth analyzing.

Why do you feel that way about it?

It will not be long before you find that
accurate daily accounts are not only an interesting record, but that they soon become
a potent corrective. If you are really interested in fortune building you will soon discover, in watching small expenditures, that
the majority of men never come to possess
a modest fortune because they drop it by
the wayside. The world to-day is full of
receptacles to catch coins for others. These
coins accumulate into vast sums. If any one
of us could contrive a mechanism that would
as regularly catch our stray coins for us, we
should rapidly find ourselves beyond the reach
of poverty.

Exactly this kind of a machine can be made
by the two processes of careful appropriation
and accurate keeping of accounts. One of
the first results of keeping accounts is that
it puts us on guard against habits of apparently trifling expenditures that are small day

by day, but enormous when carried on for a period of years. Another result, equally potent, comes from pride of accomplishment. The moment one succeeds in guarding his money, the saving account begins to grow. With its growth comes a rightful pride of possession, and a growing conviction that one is becoming master of the situation. If evil days fall, there is provision; or, in other words, by daily economy one soon secures an amount of protection that, when necessary, covers weeks and months.

A man who is strictly honest with himself will not be afraid of an account book. On one page let him write the month's total of receipts. From this total there are to be paid fixed charges—rent, for instance. Then the total of fixed charges should be subtracted from the total income for the month. An itemized account of the balance will constitute the detail of daily expenditure. Enter everything without fear, for at the end of the month the income and expense accounts should balance to a penny.

Certain expenditures are made in cash; others are paid for at the end of the month. The smaller the income, the more necessary it is to reduce monthly bills to the smallest number; and to do a cash business. In this way, a man knows exactly where he stands every night. It is easy to charge a purchase when one has not the money to pay for it. Often such a purchase can just as well as not be deferred, and one who does business on a cash basis often will defer until he is prepared to pay.

It may be found unnecessary to continue a daily cash account of expenditures after the good of the practice has been accomplished. This happens when one has forever eliminated foolish expenditures and gets down to the basis of taking pride in the saving habit rather than in the spending habit.

A few months, or a year or two, will bring about this result. You will then be provided with a true history of your habits. Eliminate the useless and unwise. Make a list of the necessary and essential.

At the end of a year or so, you can determine with a fair degree of accuracy how much you spend annually for fuel, taxes and clothing, for example. Set aside the pro rata amount monthly or weekly, and you will forever after be forehanded when these payments are required.

It is an axiom that the less one has the more it demands to be husbanded.

In a letter addressed to a newspaper, a workingman's wife asks:

"I should like to know how to build a fortune on a spasmodic income. How can I save for the future when, for five months of the year, my husband has no work?"

It is easy to save (if one knows how) on a steady income. On an income that is not steady, it is often impossible. But there are many ways by which good business methods can be applied to money that comes in now and then instead of regularly.

To begin with, no workingman's wife should be expected to pay twelve months' housekeeping out of seven months' pay. Even

with the greatest economy these two ends cannot be made to meet.

If it is right to consider a family and the
wages that come in as a business that should
be made to pay, some things are important
before everything else:

1. A fixed schedule of expense that has
been worked out carefully.

2. No extravagances to-day that will weak-
en the business six months from now.

3. Everything possible must be done to improve the business.

Thousands of women are carrying out the
first two of these conditions successfully, and
many of them get few thanks or no recog-
nition for it. They are first-class financiers
who succeed in steering the business of the
family safely when nothing but shipwreck
seems possible.

The third condition is the most difficult to
master.

What can be done to improve the business
aspect of the family? That is, what steps
can be taken to create more business?

There is more appeal to the higher qualities in human nature back of these questions than at first appears. If a man's work is of a kind that throws him into idleness five months of the year, what can he do about it?

Work of this kind plunges a family into a life of uncertainty that must stimulate a lot of guessing. Should one pin his faith to such work, or try to put himself in shape to do another sort of work that is apt to last all the year round?

Writers on social subjects have said a thousand times that anyone can, in his leisure hours, prepare himself for a better job. Whether these writers ever tried it, or not, the statement does nevertheless seem reasonable.

In a work day of eight hours, there ought to be enough time margin after all else is accounted for, to permit a man to think an hour or two for himself. This extra hour or two that most all of us can find is the very backbone of all the Correspondence School Courses. These schools have made trained

men out of the untrained, and put the pay
envelope on a fifty-two weeks' basis.

But such schools are by no means all the
opportunity a man has. In them, however,
is the one great suggestion that appeals to
every one of us: whether we are successful or
not.

It is this:

You can find some time every day for the
improvement of yourself as a worker. You
can get skill in something or other by using
your thoughts about your own future.

Spare time is as good as money to many
men. A man can look around, question, and
learn something. Anyone on the move is
pretty sure to find what he is looking for if
persistence, intelligence and learning something every day are all they are said to be.

Hence, the seven months a year workers
can only begin to build a fortune in money
by first building it in skill in spare time. The
ultimate value of spare time put in on some
one definite thing is infinitely better than a
part-time occupation.

But a part-time occupation is often a real thing. What is to be done while it lasts? Keep accounts. Manage every penny. Systematize expenditure. But all the while do everything possible to improve the working equipment. Five months of idleness out of twelve may be want and penury, or it may be opportunity.

It depends on how one looks at it.

CHAPTER V.

THE WONDERS OF INTEREST

Take care of the pennies and the pounds will take care of themselves.

The man intent on building a fortune cannot too often review the fundamental essentials. It is only by keeping them constantly in mind that he can succeed, for fortune building results, not from sporadic action but from a well thought-out plan that is constantly operative. Let us repeat these fundamental principles:

1. The builder must aim to secure such a fortune in money as lies reasonably within his opportunity.

2. He must store up mental resources as well as money.

3. Health, Skill, and Leisure are his great assets.

63

4. He must master all that is implied in appropriation and daily accounts.

5. He must constantly remember that he is working with his strength of to-day in order to protect himself in the days of lessening strength to come.

6. And he must not so slavishly attach himself to a scheme of saving that he fails to get joy from the days of his toil.

There are many ways and means of disposing of savings. We will take them up one by one, in subsequent chapters. They all, however, have one end in view; namely, to provide safety and increase. In order that savings may be safe, a depository of some kind must be found for them that is as wisely safeguarded as human ingenuity can devise. In order that they may increase, they must be left undisturbed over a period of time, for it is Time that increases the value of savings.

Thus, money is put into savings banks, into bonds, or other investments, that it may earn interest. Interest is payment made by the user of money to the man who owns it, just as rent is the payment made by the user of a house to the man who owns it. Hence, interest is cash received. Some people, particularly the French, Dutch, and Germans have become noted the world over for their thrift. One of their cardinal rules is: never spend interest; add it to principal and make it earn interest in its turn.

When savings are invested wisely and the income is husbanded, the growth of principal is truly remarkable. One dollar saved weekly for twenty years amounts to ten hundred and forty dollars as principal but if deposited regularly and never disturbed, in a savings bank that pays four per cent compound interest, this ten hundred and forty dollars will earn in twenty years, as interest, five hundred and sixty-two dollars, making a total of $1,612.00.

Small sums regularly set aside and left to work over a period of ten, twenty, or thirty years, grow to mighty sums.

If a young man begins at the age of twenty-five to save for a pension at sixty-five, that is, forty years later, each thousand dollars *of the amount he desires,* will cost him an annual deposit of ten dollars and twelve cents, at four per cent, compound interest. Or, it may be expressed thus: less than three cents a day over a period of forty years, amounts to one thousand dollars.

Everybody has the three cents, but few have forty years of patience.

At the same rate of interest, one dollar a week, deposited regularly for twenty-five years, amounts to nearly twenty-three hundred dollars.

In the first instance the thousand dollars costs four hundred and four dollars and eighty cents in money deposited. The interest adds six hundred and ninety-five dollars and twenty cents.

In the second, the total of two thousand, two hundred and fifty-two dollars costs thirteen hundred dollars, and the interest adds nine hundred and fifty-two dollars.

These are certainly encouraging and inspiring figures. Beginning with even a small sum, one can rapidly work out a fortune, on paper. But actually to work out a fortune in money requires great moral courage and strength. A man who determines to place one dollar in the savings bank every Saturday for a period of twenty years, is entering into a contract to do a series of actions one thousand and forty times. The actions are these:

1. He must get the dollar together during the week.

2. He must make up his mind to go to the bank.

3. He must put on his hat and coat and go to the bank.

4. He must never miss a trip, for if he does, the plan he has established is retarded that much.

But for all this trouble he has his rewards. And his rewards are these:

1. He is giving himself a valuable mental and moral training.

2. He is inaugurating and continuing a good habit.

The remarkable augmentation of small sums of money regularly deposited makes it plain that old age poverty is seldom neces-' sary. As a rule, old age poverty is the price paid for many years of improvidence, and of a good time to-day without thought of to-morrow. It is the result of choice made daily between having something now, and part in the future. There is no written law that can compel a wage earner to save for the pro-tection of himself and family. If he elects not to secure this protection, is it to be won-dered at that the world turns a deaf ear to his appeal for charity when he can no longer support himself and others dependent upon him?

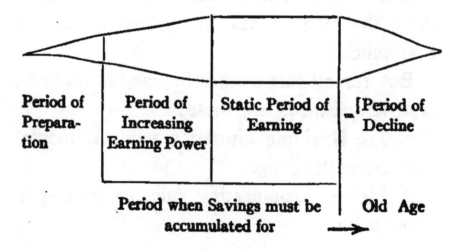

| Period of Prepara-tion | Period of Increasing Earning Power | Static Period of Earning | [Period of Decline |

Period when Savings must be accumulated for   Old Age

The art of wasting money can be learned by the poorest fool alive, but the art of husbanding it wisely for present living and future protection is the accomplishment of a man who, by his effort, has gained more and more wisdom. The cultivation and development of manhood is the one vital factor in the wise stewardship of money. So Thrift brings two essential rewards: wisdom and independence. He is an unwise man who complains of the bitterness of his own folly; and he is a wise man who determines not to buy folly to-day, for he knows he will have no use for it to-morrow.

We have spoken of the inspiration that comes from learning the interest-earning power of money. But back of this inspiration lies a cold fact. You cannot hurry the matter. That a dollar saved to-day may increase to two dollars, you must put it at work and never touch it for nearly twenty years. The man who tosses a dime over to the barkeeper is handing him all the money that a dollar bill can earn in two years when most favorably invested. One ten cent cigar every day for a year costs four per cent interest on nearly one thousand dollars. This suggests the only logical way by which a man should estimate the cost of inessential things. That is, what capital do they represent? A banker who broke down from overwork confessed to his physician that he had been in the habit of smoking twenty cigars a day. Being a well-to-do man, he paid not less than twenty-five cents each for them. Hence, his smoking cost five dollars a day. This represents five per cent interest, annually, on thirty-seven thousand, five hundred dollars. The sum itself which he spent in order to break down, namely, one thousand, eight hundred and twenty-five dollars per year, would pay the full tuition, in a small college, of thirty-six young men or women.

As small sums regularly saved amount to astonishingly large ones, so often a small business produces peculiarly significant results. Here is a case in point:

Twenty-two years ago an emigrant, a

woman, arrived in New York from Russia—with no money, and with no knowledge of the English language.

She set up a news-stand, and bent all her energy to establishing a steady business on the lines of quick service, politeness, attention to details, and knowledge of human nature.

She kept up this line of action every day of the year. And she wore a sunshiny face even when New York weather was trying to rival that of Siberia.

A little while back, she began to wonder what all the pennies she had taken in amounted to, in present assets. Here is a list of her holdings:

1. A three-story house in Brooklyn.
2. Enough money to buy the house next door.
3. Still some money left in the bank.
4. Seven children.
5. Five grandchildren.

One of her sons is an architect. All her children are self-supporting. She can, so she proudly declares, put on a fine silk dress when occasion demands. She is young in spirit and cheerful of heart.

Another of her business assets has been unfailing good nature.

And it has all been done out of a penny business. No need to worry about an old age pension—nor about old age itself, for this business woman has apparently made up her mind to keep young.

She has been giving good service in the midst of the great moving picture show of life in a great city. It has amused her, and has given her a little fortune in return.

And she is not yet sixty years of age.

To get the full force of this story, just imagine yourself going to a foreign country, with not a word of its language at your command, thirty-five years of age, entirely dependent on yourself, and making good.

The biographies in books are full of interest, but the biographies of the streets are full of inspiration.

Here is another case, of simple industry, good judgment, and a life simply expressed:

There died in Greenwich Village, New York, not long ago, a man who was a familiar figure to the entire neighborhood. When he was fourteen years old he arrived in America, from County Cork, Ireland, and he landed as poor as thousands of other immigrants.

He went to work on the South American steamboats, and not only made his body do a good day's work, but he kept his mind just as active as his hands.

In the course of time this mind of his led him to become an engineer, and becoming an engineer led him to invent various devices that proved practical.

Plain Tim, as he was always called, was apparently no man to talk much about himself. In outward appearance he continued day after day and year after year, the same man, worker, and neighbor.

Then he went into steam-fitting, which became his principal business. He was always supposed to be in fairly well-to-do circumstances. But on this subject Plain Tim was not given to dispensing any information whatever.

For a time he served as chief engineer in a building occupied by a large publication company. A few years after he left his position, or job, as he probably called it, the firm that hired him was informed that Tim, the engineer, was now owner of the building, and they were tenants of a former employé.

Then Plain Tim died. But how had he lived?

Well, he lived about like this: Simple, quiet, industrious, active of mind, not talkative of his plans or possessions, not ostentatious.

What opportunity came his way he made as much of as there was light in him. He thought more of work than of the easy chair, and was a living illustration that if a man wants to do well, all that is needed is for him to do it.

Well, Plain Tim died, and in the course

of a few days his will was offered for probate. Then Greenwich Village was amazed to learn that his estate was worth no less than three million dollars which, as anyone will admit, is a fair sized estate.

An announcement made by the Passaic (N. J.) Trust and Safe Deposit Company relates the case of a depositor who made it his custom to put small sums into the bank. This he did "every little while," merely setting aside the sums which he could have wasted in the small expenditures common to all. After eleven years of this form of savings, the depositor wanted to buy a farm. On going to the bank he found that his savings had accumulated a substantial fund, on which the interest to his credit was over five hundred dollars. The farm cost three thousand, two hundred and fifty dollars, and there was enough to his account to pay for it. All of which proves the truth of the old saying:

"If thou shouldst lay up even a little and shouldst do this often, some time even this will become great."

Franklin, wise in all things to which he turned his philosophic mind, expressed it characteristically when he said:

"If you would be wealthy, think of saving as well as getting."

An advertisement in a magazine asks: "Can you save seventeen cents a day?"

Seventeen cents a day is approximately five dollars a month (it seems more by the month, but it is not). This amount deposited, at four per cent compound interest regularly for twenty years, will amount in total deposits to twelve hundred dollars, to which there will be found added six hundred and thirty-two dollars and eighty-four cents in interest. Total: eighteen hundred and thirty-two dollars and eighty-four cents.

It is a strain to many a mind to put aside five dollars a month for twenty years. That is two hundred and forty times. But for doing it there is a bonus of six hundred and sixty dollars. And yet there is no strain in *wasting this amount by the day.*

Now, how can we catch these pennies day

by day? Let a man who tried it (and succeeded) answer. This is his letter to the cashier of a savings bank:

"It may interest you to know that I have one of the little savings banks you give out to your depositors in my own home, left there by one of your representatives several years ago. It is, in fact, one of the prized possessions of our household, as about it we have built up a complete banking institution, with myself, and my wife and children as the officers and depositors. I am the president, my oldest daughter is the vice-president, Mrs. B. is cashier, and my oldest boy is bookkeeper.

The little bank itself acts as receiving teller, each of us having certain of the self-registering coin compartments for the deposit of our savings. We each, also, have a little pass book, made by my wife from memorandum books, in which the total of our savings is entered each time they are taken for deposit in your bank. When interest is declared on our total account at your bank it is entered in proper proportion on each of our individual books. The figuring of interest is quite an absorbing procedure; and that, together with keeping account of the total accumulated savings and credits of each, gives us all much entertainment and diversion, in addition to providing a night school of banking and general commercial practice in our own home; the effect of which upon the general development of the children is noticeable."

Chapter VI

INDIVIDUAL ADMINISTRATION

Money in the pocket soon burns a hole.

The necessity for family administration, or domestic economy, has been shown in Chapter III. The lower the income, the greater the need of this, for the fundamental demands to sustain and protect life and health are incumbent on all people alike. The worst enemy to the fortunes of a family is waste. So long as it goes on unrecognized and unrestrained, no attainment of independence is possible.

It has often been said that the poorest people in the world are those of moderate incomes, and the reason alleged for this statement is this:

With an income that is more than sufficient for the purchase of actual necessities, the temptation enters to add the cost of luxuries to the cost of necessities. The rapidity with which money disappears on this basis is amazing. Thus, the purchase of an automobile, made possible only by mortgaging the household furniture, is a case in point, and a very common one. The temptation to own a car is readily yielded to if one has any visible means whatever of earning its cost, or even of making a first payment. It is said that the frequency with which automobile dealers are compelled to foreclose chattel mortgages is appalling. In making a purchase of this kind, a man not only mortgages the property he has, but he gives in pledge his future income and his peace of mind.

Undoubtedly, all forms of installment purchases are unwise. The proper handling of this question, however, belongs to wise household administration. Unless husband and wife are equally foolish and improvident, the house property will never be mortgaged for anything one is not justified in buying.

Individual administration is but a detail of

household economy.   Many a man earning a fair salary takes a greater portion of it for his own use than he is justified in doing.   But the man who is intent on working for the future independence of himself and his family, never does this.   The salaried man, or wage earner, is on the road to fortune the moment he begins to govern his personal expenses rigidly.   He denies himself to-day, only to be the possessor of greater freedom in the future.

Hence, every man who earns money which pays for the care of a family, should compel himself to live within an allowance.   He can readily determine what amount of allowance is sufficient.   Let us take Jepson's case.   He earns considerable money, which provides all necessary expenses for his wife, three children and himself.   Until quite recently, it was Jepson's habit to draw a check for cash for his own personal needs, or for what he thought were his needs.   When household expenses increased, Jepson could not quite figure out how he came to carry so small a balance. He looked through his check books for the previous twelve months, and was amazed to find that he had drawn checks in his own favor, for pocket money, to the extent of nearly sixteen hundred dollars. If someone had asked him for a detailed report of what he had done with this money, he could not have supplied it.

Then Jepson girded himself up, and determined to stop wasting cash. He made as accurate an estimate as he could of his daily and other personal expenses over a year. The list included these items: car fares, daily papers, lunches, clothing of all kinds, postage, tailoring, laundry, cigars, and monthly magazines. He figured industriously on this, in the desire to eliminate wastefulness. Finally, he determined that on an allowance of fifteen dollars per week (or seven hundred and eighty dollars per year) he could meet all his personal expenditures. So he began on this basis. At the end of the first week he had a small balance. This he put in a drawer in his desk, and in each succeeding

week he added to it the unexpended portion
of his allowance. When it accumulated to
five dollars he put it in a savings bank, opening the account in the joint names of his wife
and himself.

At the end of the first year, Jepson had a
credit account in the savings bank of one
hundred and seventy dollars. The second
year he did not set aside quite so much. This
was due to the fact that, during the first year,
he had in hand a supply of clothing which
later on had to be replenished. And yet the
second year's allowance yielded in savings
eighty dollars, making a total for two years
of two hundred and fifty dollars. This
amount, remember, he set aside not from his
income but from his personal allowance. Having determined never to trespass on his salary beyond this amount for his personal needs,
his affairs soon straightened out, and Jepson
found himself able to invest a little money
from time to time.

Thus, the simple expedient of studying his
own individual case, and of eliminating waste,

made him a good manager, and the art of good management which he learned reflected its salutary influence upon all his finances. It must be remembered that the amount involved in an operation of this kind is the fact of least value. Jepson earned a good income and was required by the demands of his business to pay for some things that a wage earner can afford to disregard. The principal value of this illustration is this: The allowance plan prevents any man, whether he earns much or little, from wasting money on himself. Generally it is wasted selfishly. The man who drinks and smokes, rarely thinks of making his wife an equal allowance that she may spend on little things, as dear to her as liquors and cigars may be to him.

An interesting story is told of a young woman who went into equal partnership with her husband, on the drink allowance.

The story may be said to illustrate the possibilities of every human being who earns any sum, however small. It shows that money in hand can be spent for so many things we

do not need that before we know it, there
is no money left.

It also shows that the old saying: "Many
a mickle makes a muckle" is a sound one.

There was a young man in Manchester,
England, who went to work in a calico-print-
ing factory. He earned good wages, and always spent his money as it pleased him, and
one of his ways was to buy beer.

On the day this young man was married
his young wife asked him to let her have
money enough to buy two glasses of beer
a day for herself. They both worked; he
going from the factory to the saloon, and
she going from the factory to put the house
in order. Occasionally this young wife was
able to get her husband to come home a little
earlier than usual and spend the hours they
had free from work with her instead of with
the men who drank beer until bedtime.

On the day they had been married a year—
their first wedding anniversary—the husband
said:

"Mary, we have had no holiday since we

were married. If I had a penny in the world I would take you to visit your mother."

It showed a good heart if not a careful man, and Mary said:

"Would you like to go, John? If so, I'll pay for the trip."

John was amazed, and said:

"How can you pay? Have you a fortune all at once?"

"No," said Mary, "but I've been saving my pint of beer."

"What?" asked John.

"My pint of beer," and with that answer Mary went to the place where she had been hiding her pennies every day and brought the price of seven hundred and thirty glasses of beer.

She placed all the money in her husband's hands, and said:

"John, we can have a holiday, and go to visit mother."

Now, the best part of the story is this: John supposed all the year that Mary was, like himself, spending her pennies for beer

that she drank day by day. When he realized what it meant to have pennies in hand,
and what it meant to have a wife like Mary,
he said:

"I'll never drink again."

And he never did. He and Mary saved
their pennies, made little investments carefully, and in a few years they had a country
home, carriage, and a factory of their own.

Mary was a blessing.

We all wish to be rich, or well-to-do, and
while we wish it we heartily curse the times
and the taxes we must pay. But, after all,
we make our own hard times, to an extent,
and the heaviest taxes are those *we impose
upon ourselves.*

John taxed himself for beer. We all pay
this tax in one way or another.

We are all of John's kind. What Mary's
thought awakened in John was not only a
sense of the worth of money, but a sense of
that which money represents. And the money
represented John's labor, strength, skill, time
and character. When he saw it in that light

he realized how easy it is for a man to be foolish.

Well, no fun, no good times, no little pleasures?

Not first. As a man's money is his character, it must be divided and paid out as character demands. First, the bills are to be paid, then the amount to be saved, lastly, the money for pleasure; and this money should bring pleasure to *all* the family, not to one member of it alone.

This kind of earning and spending does not make man a prisoner to life. It makes him free. It cultivates self-denial and self-reliance. It kills debt and the loan shark.

While Jepson could not have told what he did with sixteen hundred dollars in cash in the course of a year, it soon became evident to him where it had gone, because the influence of his allowance system inevitably caused him to study his habits. He had been wasteful in his purchases instead of frugal. He did an amazing amount of "treating" for a man in his position. It became more and more easy for him to ride into town in an automobile, at a cost of two dollars, as against using the street car at a cost of five cents. He often remained in town for dinner, not from necessity, but from a disinclination to go home after business hours. His cigar box, and, in fact, his cash in hand, were always more or less available to others. His tips were numerous and generous. In brief, he had become a popular man because his trail was marked by shining coins.

Thousands of men live the same sort of reckless financial life. Well-to-do as they may seem to be from the amount of annual salary, they are really poor from their improvident administration of it. The simple device of taking himself in hand, ultimately put Jepson and his affairs on a sound basis. He recognized that he had been wasting the very money that would make him independent. Once he became aware of this fact, he set out to possess the independence that rightfully belonged to him, and even more rightfully to his family.

A man responsible to no one but himself may play the fool and escape censure, unless the misfortune overtakes him, in later life, of being thrown upon charity. But the man who stands as the protector of a family is a criminal if he endangers that protection.

The word husband means the bond that binds the household securely. If the bond be loosed and weakened until the household falls into want and misfortune, are we not justified in calling him who permits this, a destroyer of the faith, one unworthy of the position he so eagerly sought when his heart was intent on winning the girl of his choice?

We soon discover that we actually buy money. When we want more of it, we really are in the market to buy more. Whoever wants more is wise to figure the cost, for money has its price, just as better clothes and a finer house have.

How must the worker pay for money?

A worker must pay for money in thought, skill, industry, reliability, and dependability.

Thought makes him a more careful workman; takes him farther into his business; makes him an investigator; expands him.

Skill is his prime stock in trade. On skill particularly he can set his money value. To get the most in return for what he can do, his skill must be of a kind that is in demand.

A man whose specialty is the birds of the United States may find a small market in which to dispose of his skill and knowledge. If one knows how to make an article wanted by every household, can make it better than anyone else, his market is broad and consequently richer.

Skill amounts to little without industry.

The English colliers of the last century earned high wages; but they knocked off work on Saturday night and kept out of the mines until the following Tuesday or Wednesday. That is, most of them did. Those who did not, were paid not only for their skill and industry, but for Reliability and Dependability as well.

A man or woman who earns money sets the limit. To get more means to give more, and to give more one must not be asleep under the green bay tree of self-indulgence.

CHAPTER VII

THE HOUSEHOLD EXPENSE BOOK

Bookkeeping is the history of money in motion.

Money is valuable when it is in motion. When it is hidden away in a secret place, it is not fulfilling its prime function. Money in motion reaches its highest point of efficiency when it works for a worthy object. Thus, money paid for rent, food, and clothing brings necessities to us and is active in the world of work that produces supplies.

Some students of household administration have devised what is called the household expense book. It is to be had in many forms, and all of them are, more or less, practical. The principal objects are two in number:

(1) To introduce system in the handling of money.

(2) To keep clearly before the householder *the channels through which his money must be paid to the active world about him.*

To one who takes any degree of pride in handling his affairs wisely, there is some degree of pleasure in making such a book, rather than buying it ready made. Any blank book, five by seven inches, with ledger ruling, is adaptable for this purpose. The left hand page should carry the list of all regular supplies required monthly. The right hand page should be devoted to income. This will be a single item of entry, if income is received monthly; or it will be made up of four or five entries if it is received weekly.

The main object is so to manage affairs that the sum total of items on the left shall be less than the sum total on the right. The balance is the margin of safety. It will take the householder a year to bring such a book into complete working order, for while some items occur regularly, month by month, others are irregular; for example, physicians' bills; or infrequent though regular, like the winter's supply of coal. The fundamental rule to follow in making up the list of expense units, is to admit none that is not absolutely essential. This rule should be followed by the other which requires that the account for the month shall be a true and exact history, not only of every dollar received, but of every cent.

This is not a useless burden of small care. Inasmuch as the money you earn is all you have to show for your labor, anything that concerns its wise administration is worth attention. When you discover exactly what habits you have been cultivating for a long time, that occasion you to spend even a little now and then, you will be astonished and delighted; astonished, because at first you will scarcely credit the truth of the matter; and delighted, because you will know where to begin to establish your independence.

Every family should be regarded as a business and be placed on a business basis. At first thought there may seem to be a narrow restriction in this. As a matter of fact, it is

the basis of prudence. Every family stands
in a strict business relation with many people.
The grocer may be your friend and neighbor,
but as a grocer he is a man with whom you
carry on business relations. This is made evident the moment a diagram is made showing
the channels through which the average family reaches the world outside of itself. Here
is the diagram:

INCOME TO	PAYMENTS TO
The family as a business organization.	Dry Goods and Clothing Man.
	The Landlord
	Butcher.
	Grocer.
	Baker.
	Coal and Wood Dealer.
	Ice Man.
	Wife's Allowance.
	Husband's Allowance.
	Savings Bank.

Every family must make its own list of
expense channels. These are its relations as
a business organization. It is through these
channels that the distribution of income must
be made. Every householder should make

such an outline, and on the basis of its demands apply the plan of Appropriation described in Chapter III. On this plan, as a working basis, keep the family accounts. The savings bank book keeps its own account. Neither husband nor wife will fail to benefit from the experience of accounting accurately for the distribution of the personal allowance; if any portion of it is unexpended, or if there is a falling off of any regular expense, these sums may be set aside for an amusement fund for the pleasure of the family as a whole. With such a plan in hand as a reward of responsibility, it is less likely that one will spend much money on amusements while regular business obligations (commonly called bills) are unpaid.

Every householder should take pride in this plan of campaign. It is an up-to-date record of his financial standing. The peace of mind that comes from knowing exactly how you stand is directly conducive to health. When bills are paid they are breeding neither worry nor discontent. He who can remain perpetually behind in his obligations, without discontent, is mentally unhealthy.

A man whose affairs are well in hand, who is fully aware of his responsibilities, who is not behind in his payments, whose earnings and whose plan of operation permit him to save something as a surplus, is in the position to hear the knock of Opportunity when it comes. But the man whose affairs are in disorder, who is forever struggling and yet is behind in the game, lives a life of such confusion that he is in danger of missing even the obvious opportunities. "Real opportunity," John D. Rockefeller has said, "comes only to the man with ready money."

The family expense book, and all it stands for, permits a man to keep his head up and on his shoulders where it belongs. Whether he lives on a narrow margin or a liberal one, its service has the same value. If the income be small he can watch its outgo accurately; if it be more liberal, he can save more and give his family more comforts and pleasures. But, in whatever circumstances he finds himself, there is one item that he must keep persistently before himself; that is future protection.

The time to heed this matter is Now. To eat, drink, and be merry to the full extent of the day's income, can spell only one word— Want. A mill-stone around a man's neck is a pearl necklace compared with the ultimate sorrows of improvidence.

Do not think that to regard the family as a business organization takes the joy and poetry out of it. They can enter into it in no other way. If you wish your family joy, let your business method do its share in creating it. If you want to experience the poetry of family life, do not think you can create it with a background of unpaid bills.

It has already been pointed out that the important factor, back of all financial accounts centering around the family, is the system itself and not the amount involved. Herewith there is given the actual account of income and expense of a man who has not varied from these figures for several years.

He lives fifteen miles out of New York City, commutes daily; he is married, and has one child, a boy of six. He is carrying a mortgage on a property that is taxed for about ten thousand dollars.

Total monthly income......................... $275.00

Distribution—

   a. To Mrs. Saunders............... $110.00
   b. To savings, taxes, etc........... 125.00
   c. To Mr. Saunders (personal allowance) 40.00

       Total $275.00

Detail of Appropriation

  A. Total amount........................... $110.00
    Groceries $40.00
    Maid service 20.00
    Fuel 10.00
    Clothing 10.00
    Small house expenses............ } 30.00
    Carfares and sundries........... }

                  $110.00

  B. Total amount $125.00
    Tax account $15.00
    Interest on mortgage........... 45.00
    Savings (to reduce principal on mortgage) 65.00

                  $125.00

C. Total amount $40.00
    Clothing $10.00
    Commutation 7.20
    Fares in town.................. 5.00
    Club dues 3.00
    Laundry, tailor, barber.......... 4.00
    Charity 3.00
    Lunches 7.00
                                                   $39.20
    Balance ....•..... 80
                                                   $40.00

This expense distribution is not a theory but a fact. Both husband and wife set aside monthly ten dollars each for clothing fund. The annual tax bill is provided for by setting aside its monthly pro rata. So, too, is the interest money that is paid semi-annually.

It will be noticed that no provision is made for amusements or summer vacation. The amusement fund comes from any unexpected balance in appropriations A or C. Vacations will come some day; in the meantime, the family is slowly but surely coming into possession of a home-property worth ten thousand dollars.

Another case of husband and wife, less detailed than the preceding, shows that there is a beneficial outcome in any systematic plan.

Fowler married on an income of one hundred and twenty dollars a month.

Despite the "two can live as cheaply as one" proverb, the end of the month and a depleted pocketbook were regular coincidences.

At the end of the year, as a result of the Christmas expenditure, Fowler was in debt. He went to a banker who had been a friend of his father and requested the loan of one hundred dollars. Having known the young man's father intimately, and Fowler himself from childhood, the loan was made without hesitation.

"Fred," the banker inquired, "how are you making it, now that you and Clara are married?"

Without any withholding of the facts, Fowler told the banker of his financial affairs.

"The fact is," he said, "I need more money, and in so small a town as this it is impossible to earn more."

"No," said the banker, "you don't need more money just now. It wouldn't change the top of your head nor the state of your affairs at the end of the month. What you need more than money is system.

"Now I have known you and Clara ever since you were children, and I am sure I may speak plainly, may I not?

"Very well. To begin with, I am going to sell you a first class five hundred dollar bond. Now you must pay for this bond no less than twenty-five dollars per month. At present your legitimate expenses are comparatively small. The source of your trouble is waste; waste in little things.

"Oh, yes, I know you don't think so, but that is the secret of no savings in ninety-nine cases out of a hundred. Now try the plan that I suggest. If it fails I will release you on the bond obligation.

"You draw your salary monthly, do you not? Good! On the first of January you give Clara sixty dollars and keep sixty dollars. Let her pay the maid, the house charges, and her personal expenses. You pay the rent, fuel, telephone (if you have one), and your personal accounts.

"On the last day of the month I shall expect both of you to bring me twelve dollars and fifty cents each. BOTH of you, mind you. Don't you come with twenty-five dollars. Make Clara bring her share. When husband and wife begin mutually to save, a little fortune is assured; never forget that."

Fowler remarked, afterward, that the only thing that sustained him on the way out was the hundred dollars that he had succeeded in borrowing. He went home, talked it over with his wife, found her willing to try the plan, and forthwith they began on sixty dollars a month each to face the world.

"I had two inspirations," said Fowler. "The first was that we were working together for our common good; the second was, I wanted that bond.

"The first few months we just managed to pay the twenty-five dollars. Then we began to keep a strict account of every penny expended, to eliminate all unnecessary waste, of which we found there was quite a little; and we paid for the bond and the hundred dollars I borrowed, in two years.

"The bond and its coupons inspired me to have another. We have systematized our expenses and can generally save more than twenty-five per cent of my salary."

Chapter VIII

DEBT AND THE EMERGENCY FUND

"We are creatures of habit. We succeed or we fail as we acquire good habits or bad ones; and we acquire good habits as *easily* as bad ones. That is a fact. Most PEOPLE do not believe this. Only THOSE who FIND IT OUT succeed in life."—HERBERT SPENCER.

A man in debt, however it has come about, has borrowed money. He does not owe the tailor a suit of clothes, nor the grocer a list of supplies; he owes the actual money involved in the transactions. They have really extended the money to him as a loan.

While the best advice about debt is Punch's famous dictum—Don't! it is often impossible to avoid it in a measure. So customary has it become, for example, to carry certain fixed charges on "monthly account," that merchants regard monthly payments, if promptly made, as equivalent to cash. If a strictly cash business is impossible, debt should proceed no further than the regular monthly account.

Probably the number of families that, by forethought, adhere to the rule of prompt monthly payments and no debts, is comparatively small. When they become entangled with bills they cannot pay, with the loan shark and the like, the high cost of living comes in for another hearty denunciation. It is a handy excuse, but it is not always valid. Much debt is contracted that has nothing to do with the cost of living as made necessary by economical family administration.

Recent efforts in New York, and elsewhere, to legislate the loan shark out of business, brought forth many pitiful cases of borrowing that were apparently made necessary by dire circumstances. The way, of course, to avoid such conditions, is to prepare for them. One who has paid a loan shark ninety dollars for a loan of thirty, is certainly to be sympathized with; but even he may look back to days before he found himself so hard pressed, and recall not a few instances of expenditures that he must repent in the days of trouble.

It should be sufficient to say: Do not bring debt upon yourself. Yet it is hard, if not quite impossible, for one to realize in the days when Want does not pinch, that a little care then will keep one from the misfortune of the usurer's game. Once again, it must be repeated that the whole philosophy of money is: Spend less than you earn. Better the restriction of frugal economy for years, than a few months of being pursued by a pitiless creditor.

It has, indeed, been well said that he who does not spend all he earns is a capitalist.

All advice that may be given about possible future debt is summed up in the words: Always be preparing for it. Unexpected expenditures fall upon all of us. It is on the occasion of their arrival that we realize their meaning. Many a family encounters what seems, and virtually is, a catastrophe when obligations come and there has been no anticipation.

It should be the aim of every householder to build up an Emergency account. He may not need it for years, but if the need comes and there is nothing in hand, one wishes that he had stinted himself unmercifully to be prepared for what has happened. A small account paid up regularly as insurance against the unexpected is an absolute family necessity. Put aside a few cents or a dollar a week, any sum you can, but do it with regularity. Keep it in a safe place. Even a year may go by and no call be made upon it, but when it does come, have this home made accident policy ready to help. You will never know the independence and comfort there are in it, until you have been caught without it.

Loan shark borrowing is seldom resorted to except in extreme measures. Borrowing "between friends," as "man to man," and so on, is common. A man who borrows among his friends, gradually extending the circle of his indebtedness, may have been born a gentleman, but he is rapidly losing the characteristics of one. Even if a man becomes so

skillful in doing it that it gives him no con-
cern, he should have enough sense to realize
that his habit is the common talk of his acquaintances.

Friendly borrowing is an unmistakable
sign of improvidence. When it runs from
week to month, and from month to year, it
destroys confidence, and the bonds of friendship are broken. Then the borrower criti-
cizes his friend and openly complains of him.
In brief, he curses one who pays toll for him
over the bridge.

A chronic borrower is a paradoxical object.
He attends his clubs, smokes good cigars, pursues the pleasures of life, and regards obligations lightly, apparently oblivious that his
honor is involved.

The summation of the matter is:

1. Have as few charge accounts as possible.

2. Pay them promptly every month, or
whenever due.

3. Build up an emergency fund, remem-
bering it is the anchor that will hold you

secure some day when you are in troubled waters.

4. Avoid the loan shark as you would avoid pestilence.

5. Do not borrow from your friends. You cannot afford to pay the price in wrecked reputation.

6. Whether money buys necessities or pleasures for you, see that you get your money's worth.

7. Your friend is no longer a friend if you cannot pay what you owe him. And, after all, friendship is above the price of material things.

8. Any man can keep out of debt who lives within his income.

9. Better a frugal life than the foreclosure of a chattel mortgage.

10. Better lend than borrow, but do neither if you can avoid it.

Here follows the story of how one woman found her way out of the debt situation:

We were forever struggling to pay last month's bills—and some of the month before.

It made me so weary to buy to-day's supplies with those overdue charges in view that I didn't enjoy my meals.

Fortunately we had a little money in the savings bank, which, despite our debts, we had clung to as a veritable life-preserver. My husband's pay came in once a month and it was enough—if we only had known it.

One month-end, it was the 30th of May, I made up my mind to break my rule about not touching the savings bank account. I drew out all but ten dollars, paid every bill, took the pay envelope of eighty-five dollars for May, and made up my mind that thereafter we should live by rule rather than by accident. So I made a budget, putting down every *regular* item of expense. I knew we could stand that. I suspected that our trouble grew out of *irregular* items. And I was right.

When I was sure I had everything on my list that belonged there, I set against it the amount it called for, if the charge was a fixed one. On others that varied from month to month I allowed enough. The total amount was nearly seventy-four dollars. The eleven dollars went to the savings bank at once to begin to make up the withdrawal.

Then I paid the June bills as they fell due and found at the end of the month that my estimate of seventy-four dollars was over three dollars too much. I put this aside against a possible deficit in the next month's account.

This plan has worked perfectly, and for the reason that we now pay from the budget list and not from a notion that we can afford anything that strikes our fancy.

Anyone who will try this plan will get out of trouble. It is just a sensible way of keeping your own accounts. It means spending by system.

The way to do it? Well, what I do is to rule off a sheet of paper every month. This is no trouble. And then I make a list of items. Against each item I put the exact amount required, or as near it as past experience tells me is right.

Then I pay every bill promptly.

And I never forget that any balance belongs to the savings bank at the end of the month.

It is easy enough. If you ever run short, the savings account is ready to help. A rainy day fund is like an umbrella, it is all right to put it up when the rain comes.

Now debt is not infrequently, perhaps it generally is, a symptom of wrong methods. It spells wrong thought, wrong ideas about money earned and spent; in short, a wrong mental condition. As savings and economy must begin in thought, so debt must be avoided by thought, for it is everlastingly true that as a man thinketh in his heart *so is he*. If he thinks debts, they come to him.

"The best use of money," says the proverb, "is to pay bills." The American writer, Ralph Waldo Emerson, sums it up tersely when he says: "Spend for Power and not for Pleasure." He means that a man can increase himself if he spend wisely; he can buy things of real value to himself, and not alone the foolish things that merely keep on repeating the old round of animal sensation.

Again this writer points out: "The estate of a man is only *a larger kind of body.*" If his body wants drink, drink becomes his estate; and his estate is soon debt-involved; because, it is drink-involved. If a man wants to live in the comfort and content of a well-ordered life, he will spend with system. And once he learns that, he will always be prepared for debt and never buried beneath it.

Once in debt, however, what is to be done? First of all let us not be cowardly, but ascertain the extent to which we are in arrears. We are as one lost in the woods; the great question is: How shall we get out into the clearing? Manifestly, not by standing still; not by running around in a little ring. Effort must be aroused *and directed.*

"Let every man have the fortitude to look his affairs in the face—to keep an account of his items of income and debts, no matter how long or black the list may be. He must know how he stands from day to day, to be able to look the world fairly in the face. Let him also inform his wife, if he has one, how he stands with the world. If his wife be a prudent woman, she will help him to economize his expenditure, and enable him to live honorably and honestly. No good wife will ever consent to wear clothes and give dinners that belong, not to her, but to her shop-keeper." *

———

* Dr. Samuel Smiles.

Chapter IX

GETTING RICH IN A HURRY

The day of small things is better than that of great expectations.

In the year 1911, the United States post office department investigated a number of get-rich-quick concerns that did business through the mail. They had succeeded in collecting from the public the sum of seventy-seven million dollars in twelve months. Practically nothing of value was given in exchange. This means that while the high cost of living played havoc with slender purses, the owners of these same purses poured out seventy-seven million dollars in the expectation of becoming rich in a day, or a month, or a year. A good many gentlemen, hitherto of stylish appearance, are now in prison indicted for playing this game. And a good many more are not there who deserve to be. The tragedy back of this vast amount of money is its source. It was not given up by bankers and brokers, but by poor people, who could ill afford to lose it. And another phase of the tragedy is this: they were hypnotized into parting with their money for a purpose of which they had absolutely no knowledge; a purpose that was in every case too unreasonable to be thought of for a moment.

It would seem that the people in the humble walks of life are able to contribute collectively a large amount of money to an enticing enterprise. It is equally clear that they invariably lose their money.

Why?

1. They are tempted by greed to get much for little.

2. They make no thorough examination of the proposition.

3. Hence, they know nothing about it.

4. They fail to recognize the true function of money invested.

It must be remembered that the seventy-

seven million dollars referred to above, is
by no means all that the people of the United
States dropped into a bottomless pit in 1911.
This was the amount of transactions that
came within the province of the post office
department to consider.   How much more
went into the same pit through other channels, no one can tell.   It doubtless amounted
to one or two hundred millions of dollars.
The conclusions from this are very evident,
and they are these:

1. A large number of people have money to
invest.

2. They do not know what to do with it.

Manifestly, they are in dire need of a few
simple rules and observations about the use
of their own money.   And here they are:

1. It is impossible to get large returns on
money in a short time.

2. The first thing to be assured of before
investing money, is the reliability of the men
who invite it.

3. Then the reliability and security of their
enterprise.

4. If the men and the enterprise are all that can be desired, your money will earn approximately four and a half to six and a half per cent.

5. Many people are content to buy investments that yield even less than the four and a half per cent. *They purchase safety of principal.*

6. Some people invest money in business enterprises that yield six and a half per cent., or even a little more. *They* take what is known as the business man's risk.

7. What can a person of limited means do?

(a) He can deposit his savings in a savings bank. (The conditions for doing this are discussed in Chapter XI.)

(b) He can purchase life insurance as a protection.

(c) He can purchase wisely selected real estate.

(d) He can buy, as his savings bank account permits it, a hundred dollar bond of a reputable broker.

8. Even these conservative ways of investing money must be scrutinized. Why?

(a) As to savings banks: These are safeguarded in a few states. Select one of the best, even though you have to make your deposits by mail.

(b) Some life insurance companies are as solid financially as human ingenuity can make them. Patronize this kind alone.

(c) Some real estate is so situated as to become a constantly depreciating investment. It should be bought with judgment for appreciation.

(d) Some hundred dollar bonds are not worth the price it costs to engrave them. Hence, every bond to which savings are transferred, should be examined with infinite care.

These facts simply show that the people have millions to give to unscrupulous promoters, and that they do give them because they do not stop to consider the need of safeguarding principal. Now, the average earner, or salaried man, cannot always determine the value of an investment opportunity. He is without experience in the matter, and the conditions are so many and so complex that he cannot master them. His obvious duty then is to get information from the most reputable sources. Bankers of this high order are always willing to advise a possible client, even if he be the purchaser of only a small amount of securities.

The oft quoted instances of great estates increasing in value seem impressive when the original amount of invested money is compared with its present value. The Astor estate to-day is worth over one hundred millions, because one of the principal factors in its history is *a long period of investment accretion.* The Astor estate has not been made over night. The foundations of it were laid in the early part of the last century. Discretion and Time are the great money makers.

Another phase of the get-rich-quick experience is seldom considered. Here is a concrete instance. In 1902, a man invested ten thousand dollars in a mining proposition. After a brief and stormy existence the company went into the hands of a receiver, and all the stockholders lost the full amount of stock subscription. Taking the case of one of them, the man who invested ten thousand dollars, it would seem that this amount represents his total loss. To correct this impression we have only to ask what he would have to-day had be placed that amount in a conservative five per cent investment, say a bond. In ten years his ten thousand dollars would have earned him in interest, five thousand dollars, and in interest on interest, at five per cent, and not compounded, one thousand, three hundred and seventy-five dollars, making his total sixteen thousand, three hundred and seventy-five dollars. Now, the value of this sum at five per cent, is eight hundred and eighteen dollars and seventy-five cents annually. We may appreciate a little more clearly the full extent of his loss from the following. It consists of four items:

1. He lost his principal ten years ago......... $10.000
2. He lost ten years' interest on the principal   5,000
3. He lost ten years' interest on the interest..   1,375
_____
4. He lost a total of........................ $16,375

But! He has also lost the income on this total for all years to come. In other words, it is now costing him annually eight hundred and eighteen dollars and seventy-five cents for having been unwise ten years ago.

Mines and certain other investments seem to offer opportunities for remarkable returns. The returns are, in truth, often very remarkable. But they are certainly not very desirable.

Hence when a man comes to you with an enticing proposition, one that will double and treble your money, do not sign on the dotted line. Go to a banker of integrity and buy a security that can only double in cash value to you by means of five per cent interest for twenty years or so.

Who, then, may speculate?

1. Not the man whose current expenses are even occasionally in excess of his income.

His financial boat is approaching the falls of a financial Niagara.

2. Not the man whose current expenses absorb his entire income—crumbs, crusts, and all. His financial boat is slowly moving out to sea.

3. Not the man who has but a small margin over and above his current expenses. His business is to batten down the hatches and keep the cargo safe. He must carry ample life preservers in the form of insurance in order to protect his passengers; that is, his wife and children.

4. Here is the man who may speculate: The one who can (and does) pay all current expenses promptly; whose family is abundantly safeguarded by the most conservative form of protection; who still has over and above these requirements a surplus that he can cast into the sea without punching holes in the bottom of the boat to do it.

Once the majority of American families (and there are about fifteen millions of them) establish themselves on this basis there will be fewer panics and no more hard times.

Let us look at the matter in this way :—

Gross income........ { a. Current expenses.
b. Protection.
c. Surplus.

Get current expenses down to a reasonable basis.

Pay for protection as a current expense.

Then your surplus—if you have one—may win you a fortune when stocks are sagging and hopes are high.

"There is an idea among investors, especially those residing at a distance from New York, that it is an easy matter to pick up a good bond yielding returns of from 5 to 6 per cent. It is well known, of course, that the strictly high grade issues of the best railroads in this country are selling on a basis very close to 4%, and that the farther one gets away from this the greater the proportionate risk.

"It should not be inferred from this statement, however, that 4½% income cannot be obtained without jeopardizing one's principal, as there are a large number of issues dealt in on the New York Stock Exchange which yield approximately 4½% on the investment and which at the same time are safe for all practical purposes: in fact, one can get 5%, or even as high as 5½%, and still come within the limit of reasonable safety.

"To be sure, investments of this character do not embrace what are termed gilt-edged bonds, but when the obligation is that of a very strong company earning and paying large dividends on its capital stock, it will be seen that the risk is not a hazardous one.

"To go beyond 5½% is a step in the dark which none but the foolhardy will care to take. It goes without saying that in attempting to get 5½%, or even 5%, one should exercise considerable care in making a selection and only the obligations of the best companies should be considered, or else it should be ascertained that the collateral securing the bond is good." *

* Henry Clews.

CHAPTER X

WASTE

Waste not, want not.

Any misuse of money is a crime. Hence it is a crime to pay over savings to a man who has acquired the habit of looking honest, and at the same time, telling you that he can invest your money so that you will receive a return of twenty per cent a month on it. The human countenance is amenable to a high degree of training, and this is a notable instance of it.

But the get-rich-quick scheme is not the only means by which a worker can lose his money. Such efforts often come within the reach of the law when one man attempts to work them on another. They are outside the pale of the criminal law, however, *when a man tries to work them on himself*. This peculiar violation of the law is a moral one. It happens, on the one hand, when a man so uses money that he sets it to do impossible things; on the other, when he voluntarily disposes of it without receiving a just value in return.

All such efforts as appropriation, account keeping, administering one's personal and family affairs are correctives that aim to reveal where waste is going on, and to make it possible to eliminate it. It would seem unnecessary to suggest to a purchaser of anything that he should secure as great value for his money as he can with justice to himself and the other man. And yet the habit of care and circumspection underlying this simple act is rarely acquired. Hence, it would seem to be true that all of us are wasters of money to a degree.

When money is expended for the necessities of life, it should buy primarily, good value. This means clothing for good wearing quality, food capable of providing the highest degree of nourishment, a house so built that the honest work and reliable quality of material will assure years of efficient service. Hence, a purchase aiming to secure what we commonly call "our money's worth," involves conviction, examination, and judgment; conviction that we actually need it, that it has a part to play in the economy of our daily life; examination, that we are assured of the sterling quality of the thing itself; judgment that convinces us through examination, of the need, quality, and purpose of the thing.

Broadly stated, all money not so spent is wasted. The subject of waste is paramount over all others in domestic economy; it should be no less paramount in the administration of one's personal allowance. When its importance is recognized in these two applications, then waste disappears.

Money is wasted not only in being unwisely spent, but when the thing it has purchased is not availed of to the full extent of its utility. It has been said that the best index of domestic economy is the contents of the garbage pail. Previous generations were wiser than the present in this. The family was more intimately concerned in the value of its domestic supplies. Greater value attached to all items of personal property. The phraseology of old wills proves this: "I bequeath my Bible and my brown suit to my nephew." One can imagine how a nephew, in these days, would feel to inherit a book and a second-hand suit of clothes. Yet in former times, the Bible and the brown suit were valued *for their permanent usefulness.* They were not held in little esteem.

Purchasing wisely for utility is, however, a plan of very elastic nature. Flowers for the home seem as substantial a purchase to a lover of beautiful surroundings, as good food does to one whose appetite is hearty. But wholesome food should come first. Many a person buys jewelry who is not substantially clothed. And yet, jewelry is often a logical purchase, but only after necessities have been assured. A beautiful picture can contribute an infinite amount of pleasure to an art-loving family—but if it be purchased at the expense of proper clothing and protection against the inclemency of the weather, an inverted order has been followed in place of a direct one.

This leads to a suggestion that is probably followed to its natural conclusion by only a few people, and yet when once followed, it automatically sets things in order and never once do we begin to buy jewels and pictures when we should be purchasing necessary clothing and other like essentials. The moment affairs begin to shape themselves, and the requisite way to live is established—namely, within the income—every member of the family should be gradually supplied with his essential equipment. A workingman has to have working clothes and a best suit; hats and shoes for work and for leisure; an adequate supply of linen; warm outer covering for cold weather; rubbers or strong shoes for stormy weather, and so on. There is no worker who cannot, taking a year into consideration, make up a list of the things he actually needs. Let him, his wife and children make their lists, and, as circumstances permit, let each one own his required equipment of personal supplies. Now, if every item be purchased for durability, and be cared for adequately and renewed when it is worn out, the waste of buying inessential things before the necessities are secured, will be avoided. Then the house may be beautified, and after that, other luxuries may have their place if they do not infringe upon the one essential aim—to provide for the future.

Richard Savage with his bright scarlet coat and torn boots is a picture we seldom see now literally. But substantially, the streets of our cities abound in just such reckless incongruity. Many a man drinks and smokes the money he owes other people. Many a woman will put up with a shabby home to avoid a shabby wardrobe. All these evidences of maladministration are symptoms of trying to keep up some appearance by concealing others. The man whose foolish pride buys an automobile at the cost of a chattel mortgage, sports the machine in the eyes of his neighbors but he hides the mortgage for a while. His friends may envy him the luxury of a car, but he feels no comfort when he stops seriously to consider that its cost is reckoned in the terms of the family furniture.

A man can be sent to prison for the wrong use of the funds of other people, but he can misappropriate his own funds in countless ways, and escape the law of the land.

But he does not escape the law of retributive justice. This generally catches him when he is not expecting it, and it grips hard and unrelentingly.

Waste is an insidious disease. It creeps not only into the daily run of money, but into business and all that concerns it.

A well-known business agency makes the statement that the majority of failures are due not to hard times, competitive conditions, or the general state of trade, but to the men themselves who run the business.

A merchant to whom this statement was submitted said this:

It is probably true that most business failures lie at the door of the men themselves. In my experience, he continued, the common causes of failure are these: First, on starting a new business the founder does not look far enough ahead. The consequence is he runs out of money almost as soon as he begins. It is easy to get a new business under way, hard to keep it going until it is established.

Next: The man himself must not be a general supervisor alone, but this and a hard worker as well. He must positively know every detail of all operations that go toward bringing in money.

The young man going into business for himself must be an economist. And in two ways. Not only must every operation of his work be performed at the lowest possible cost, but he must be willing HIMSELF to economize in his private affairs. The non-observance of this single rule has bankrupted many a good beginning. Then again, let the young man going into business for himself keep his mind

forever intent on his health, his credit, his
reliability and his word.

Health undermined by foolish habits kills
industry.

Credit is established on character—let him
build character as hard as he tries to build
business.

Reliability means promptness, satisfaction
to the customer, honest product and fair price.

A man's word when it is not equivalent to
a signed bond, is a house built on sand instead
of on a rock.

The newspapers have done and are continuing to do a great service in warning the
public of fake investments. No one knows
how many people have bought building lots
in swamps full of alligators; or shares in
mines located two thousand miles away, mere
holes in the ground, as Mark Twain has said,
that are owned by a liar.

There is no distance that lends more en-
chantment than that of an investment far
away. They are always far away, always
offered to people who cannot afford to inves-

tigate them, always expensively advertised and always full of promises that are entertaining to read.   Never buy, says a writer, what you cannot see or investigate, particularly lands and mining stock.   There is plenty of good land and some good mines, but they are never advertised by a man who walks the streets with a bell; nor by the man who assures you that he is "letting you in on this as a personal favor."   The chances are he is letting you in on a big and sorrowful surprise.

This is one form of Waste that is unlawful in the eyes of both State and Federal governments.   The law punishes men who receive money under false pretences, but it cannot get the money back for you.

CHAPTER XI

THE SAVINGS BANK

The savings bank is the poor man's friend.

"If we would seek the nucleus of the savings bank," writes W. H. Keiffers, Jr. in the *Bankers' Magazine*, "especially the mutual or trustee type, it will doubtless be found in the 'sick and aid' or other friendly societies which have existed for centuries in many parts of Europe. Groups of workmen, in order to provide for the time of need, to insure decent burial, or properly to celebrate Christmas, or other festivals, were wont to form themselves into groups or associations. A small amount in dues was required, and these accumulations, together with the profit arising from social features, balls, etc., provided funds from which a small sick or funeral benefit was paid."

Any institution that offers men the opportunity of providing for the future from daily wages set aside, as deposits, is in reality a savings bank. This form of mutual beneficial institution is not an old one. Only recently the centenary of what is supposed to have been the first savings bank was celebrated in the little town of Ruthwell, in the south of Scotland.

Few if any banks for this purpose existed in Europe before the nineteenth century. It has been recorded that Henry Duncan, a Presbyterian clergyman of Dumfriesshire, organized that first bank, and by his writings did much to spread the idea. The beginning was so small that at the end of three years the deposits were only two hundred and forty-two pounds—an eloquent reminder of the comparative youth of many of the most beneficent institutions of the age in which we are living.

The savings bank in America dates from 1816, when one was established in Boston and one in Philadelphia. They are both still in existence.

The Boston institution was the pioneer of the splendid mutual savings bank system of New England, where the affairs of each bank are managed by a board of unpaid trustees, and the policy of local investments is adhered to whenever practical. Such a system has unquestioned advantages over the joint stock savings banks.

There are now more than fifteen hundred savings banks in the United States, over ten million depositors and deposits exceeding four hundred billion dollars.

In foreign lands the depositors number ninety-two millions, and the deposits are nine and one-third billion dollars.

It is hard to overestimate the importance of the lessons of economy and thrift taught the masses of the people by the institution which is still less than a century old.

To-day the savings banks are one of the best known institutions in the United States. Nearly eleven million depositors are using them. In many states the most stringent laws have been enacted to insure the safety of money to savings bank depositors. These laws specify exactly how the depositor's money shall be invested by the bank in order that it may be made to earn the expenses of carrying on business as a public benefit and also to earn the interest paid to the depositor.

As a rule the interest rate is three, three and a half, or four per cent. Money may be deposited at any time and—with certain restrictions—it may be withdrawn at any time.

On opening an account with a savings bank the depositor is required to sign the bank's rules and regulations, giving sufficient information about himself and his family to make identification easy and accurate.

The following extracts from the by-laws of a savings bank in New York, present conditions more or less common to all well-organized institutions.

1. Deposits of one dollar to three thousand dollars may be received from any single depositor.

2. On making the first deposit, the depositors shall be required, to subscribe to, and thereby signify their assent to, the Regulations and By-laws of the bank.

3. Persons not residing in the city may open accounts in writing, carefully attested.

4. On making the first deposit, every depositor shall receive a pass-book, which shall contain an extract of the By-laws and Regulations of the bank, and without the production of which [pass-book] subsequent deposits shall not be received.

5. All deposits and drafts [money withdrawn] shall be immediately entered in the books of the bank and the pass-book of the depositor. The bank is not liable to make any payment until the pass-book is handed in for the purpose of entering the payment. The bank will assume no responsibility for remittances of money to depositors.

6. Ordinarily the deposits shall be repaid on demand, but the bank may require a notice of not exceeding sixty days before such payment.

7. In case of the loss of a pass-book, notice thereof shall be given, at the depositor's expense, once a week for two consecutive weeks, in one or more of the daily newspapers. The pass-book may then be considered void and of no value, and the bank may, after two weeks have passed from the last advertisement, make payments without having the pass-book produced. The bank may, moreover, demand satisfactory security.

8. In case of the death of a depositor the bank will pay the amount due to him to his legal representatives.

9. Interest will be credited semi-annually on the first of January and the first of July, at such rate as the Board of Directors may determine, out of the earnings, on all sums of five dollars and upwards (not exceeding three thousand dollars), then in the bank, which had been deposited three or six months before such January or July.

10. Interest so credited will draw interest [as principal] from the first day of January or July, or will be paid on demand on or after

the twenty-first day of January or July respectively.

All saving banks have similar Rules and Regulations. Their one and only purpose is to safeguard the depositor and his money. Every depositor should thoroughly familiarize himself with the conditions under which money is received and re-paid.

When the first deposit has been made, the depositor should determine upon a safe place for the keeping of his pass-book; he should also note its number and be prepared, in case of loss, thus to identify it.

Savings banks are so numerous and it is so simple a matter to transact business with them that there is no need for anyone to keep a considerable fund of money in the house. Many people have lost money aggregating vast sums who have kept it in insecure places.

With greater and greater attention paid to laws enacted to protect the money of depositors in savings banks, losses through the failure of an institution are becoming fewer.

Losses through the dishonesty of bank officials are also comparatively rare; so rare in fact that they are quite a negligible quantity.

Many people hesitate to open a savings bank account thinking that small accounts are not welcomed. They are welcomed. It is a good plan to let the small coins one can save accumulate at home until one dollar is reached, then to deposit the dollar. Few of us place the proper valuation on small coins. The presence of the penny-in-the-slot machine attests their value.

This machine is a proposition, generally dealing with a copper one cent piece. We are all familiar with it, and most of us think we know what it is worth.

But we do not.

One of them saved daily for twelve months will turn into a new derby hat or a pair of shoes.

It all depends on whose slot machine gets the pennies, yours or the other man's.

With an impulse to push a penny into a

slot, why is it not worth while to have a small slot machine in the house?

One can have just as much pleasure pushing the penny in at home as if one were doing it somewhere in town.

Of course there is a difference. In town you push in the penny and get the reward at once.

At home you have to wait. But, if by waiting you can pull out a garment for one of the children, or a pair of shoes for yourself, or a day's excursion out into the country for the whole family, your machine is worth something, worth more, in fact, than the gum you chew, on other days.

When we are told that cigars and liquors cost us annually an amazing number of millions, the news does not affect us a particle. The sum is too large. We don't believe that there ever was so much money.

So the convincing way is to start at the other end and learn the actual power of pennies. They certainly have an amazing force *when they are kept together.*

Pennies are weak only when they are scattered.

A young man who leaves fifteen cents on a counter every morning for something he does not really need would be amazed if he accumulated this daily amount, say for twelve months.

The sum total would take him to Europe—second class—and lots of good people go that way.

Somebody once made a statement that made everybody else laugh, but he was right.

What he said was this:

It's the easiest thing in the world to be well off. All you have to do is to begin with pennies.

When a nation becomes thrifty throughout its social strata, the small coins must necessarily represent an important factor in producing the aggregate of wealth. A thrifty nation is a tremendous financial force when the call comes. C. H. Coffin has illustrated this fact in the *Bulletin of the American Institute of Banking:*

Prior to the war of 1870 the entire soil of France was owned by about forty thousand people. The land is now owned by between eight and ten million people, nearly all men; the women buy government bonds or such foreign securities as are offered by French bankers and approved by the authorities. Thus everyone has a stake in the country, and the tendency is toward a growth of conservatism.

At the close of the war of 1871, when Bismarck demanded the payment of an indemnity to Germany of one thousand million dollars, he supposed he had permanently crippled the French people. To the astonishment of the world the people went down into their private reservoir of cash and answered the appeal of the Government by paying in this sum, receiving in exchange therefor 5 per cent rentes. These rentes or Government bonds are unlike ours, having no date of maturity. The war was followed by a period of economy and a great increase in production. Germany was debauched by the great sum of money

poured into it and embarked upon a period of
speculation and extravagance which eventually
caused a crash and a long period of depression. France continued to gain wealth and to
have its wealth divided among the people in
a most remarkable way.

Naturally an American would suppose a five
per cent bond would be called in and paid
off at once, but no French Government ever
proposed to do this, it being thought due to
the people who came to the rescue that they
continue to receive the five per cent interest
for which they laid down their money.

In short, the French investor invariably
combines investment with patriotism and puts
his money where it will enable him to control
something in the interest of his country or to
exercise an influence upon another country in
favor of France.

The following true incident will show how
one family uses the savings bank as a part of
the family business:

My salary is moderate. I work for a corporation, and though I have heard all corpora-

tions condemned, the one I serve has been good to me and to the rest of the men.

I have learned a little about corporation rules and system, and some time ago I made up my mind that I would regard my family as a corporation and have a set of by-laws for doing business.

Here is what I wrote out:

1. Regard yourself as a corporation.

2. Vote to have no bonded indebtedness if it can be avoided.

3. Never create a bonded indebtedness without agreement of all your company.

4. Make up your Net Quick Assets every month.

5. Keep Net Quick Assets in hand to a value approximating annual expenses for one year.

6. Create a Cash Sinking Fund during ten years, of ten per cent of each year's gross receipts.

7. Appraise your property annually.

8. Keep a strict monthly record of Expenditures and Receipts.

9. Keep a strict list of charge accounts; and pay monthly.

10. If possible, never allow overdues.

11. Keep a strict account of Personal Expenses until they become automatic.

12. Keep a Personal Property Account, and do not buy what you do not need because it is cheap.

In regard to these rules, let me say that all I was aiming for was a plan—some sort of order that would make me systematic.

By observing Rule 3, we bought a little place carrying a mortgage, but before doing so I discussed it with my wife and her father, who lives with us, and we all voted for it.

We kept to Rule 4. By Rule 5, we have saved a little money that I get extra, as royalty on an invention. It does not pay much, but we have it all in the savings bank.

Rule 6 simply means that ten per cent of my salary is saved every month. Sometimes when expenses occur that we do not expect we have to draw on the savings account. But the main fact here *is that we have a savings account on which to draw.* I have always maintained that a saving is an umbrella to be used on a rainy day.

By Rule 10, I simply mean that we let no bills run behind. When they are due we pay them.

Rule 11 bothered me a bit. I settled the matter by making my wife Treasurer of the Corporation, and she gives me a weekly allowance. Some men smile at me for this, but it works because my wife and I are partners. I earn the money, but she works as hard as I do (and I think most wives do) and so she is a corporation member, owning half the stock. Hence she has a voice in its affairs.

CHAPTER XII

THE SAVINGS BANK AND OTHER INVESTMENTS

The forehanded man buys content and distributes it to others.

An officer of a wealthy corporation made the statement recently that of all the money he had invested over a long period of years that left in the savings bank had yielded the best results. He further specified the following reasons:

1. The safety of the savings bank.

2. The remarkable power of compound interest, if given time to work.

3. The simplicity of making deposits.

4. The possibility of depositing any sum, however small.

As a rule, the savings bank limits any single account. This is generally three thousand dollars. When this sum is reached the depositor opens an account in another bank. Hence there is practically no limit to the amount that may be thus deposited.

Not all people who save give the savings bank first place in their plan of operation. The use made of it by another investor illustrates this.

He earns a fair income, owns his home, and can put aside regularly about sixty dollars per month. For a number of years he has followed this plan:

1. On the tenth of the month, say of January, to pay all current bills. These include all accounts for the preceding month received on January first; the pro rata amounts for such expenses as taxes and fuel; his personal allowance and the allowance for his wife.

2. He carries in the Atlas Savings Bank an account of two hundred dollars *as emergency cash.* The purpose of this deposit is to serve as insurance against any unexpected expense. Should a portion of it be so demanded, he regards its use *as a loan* which he extends to

himself and repays it as he would to anyone else.

3. All other savings (which approximate sixty dollars a month) are deposited in the Citizens' Savings Bank. When the deposit amounts to seven hundred dollars he purchases a bond in the denomination of five hundred dollars, keeping a regular deposit of two hundred dollars in this bank.

4. Both savings bank accounts are in the joint names of himself and his wife.

5. As bond coupons fall due he deposits them as cash in the Citizens' Savings Bank, and they in turn augment the amount that is devoted to bond purchase.

In this particular instance the man is of the well-to-do type. In the fund referred to as "emergency cash," we find a suggestion that should be followed by the humblest householder. In the history of every family, the occasion is sure to arise when money is needed that cannot be spared from current income. Every family that, even by the practice of the severest economy and self-denial, can put aside even a few dollars, is insured against what often seems, and only too frequently is, a financial disaster.

Many a family will run along in its affairs for a year or two without encountering any but the regular expenses. This run of what is commonly called easy times or good luck is apt to entice people into spending all they have in the mistaken idea that times will always be as easy and luck always as good. But if human affairs are noted for anything it is for their variation. The hint of good times is: Be prepared. Even as little as three, four, or five dollars a month will in two years accumulate into a fund that is worth while; that may be enough or nearly enough, to help a family out of an unexpected bad situation.

Five dollars a month may seem little or much, but no one knows the actual force of it until it has been put to work. Sixty dollars a year, deposited in advance, and earning compound interest at four per cent, will work to a practical end for a depositor. For example:

1st year,	Principal and Interest			....	$62.40
2d "	"	"	"	....	127.32
3d "	"	"	"	....	194.76
4th "	"	"	"	....	264.96
5th "	"	"	"	....	337.98
6th "	"	"	"	....	408.48
7th "	"	"	"	....	492.84
8th "	"	"	"	....	574.98
9th "	"	"	"	....	660.36
10th "	"	"	"	....	749.16

We often look over a series of figures like this and say to ourselves: "I could never save seven hundred and forty-nine dollars and sixteen cents! That is more than I can spare."

The obvious answer to this objection is this:

You are not called upon to save seven hundred and forty-nine dollars and sixteen cents. All you have to do is to save *regularly*, about sixteen cents a day *and the seven hundred and forty-nine dollars and sixteen cents will take care of itself.* The depositor needs to be regular only so far as the small amount is concerned, then the big amount becomes automatic.

But suppose one has saved five dollars a month regularly for three years and then the necessity arises for money. With this thrifty observance behind it, the family has nearly two hundred dollars, to meet the emergency. And that, by the way, is the one and sole purpose of an emergency fund.

All people who save have what may be called "saving tricks" or "devices." One will put aside every nickel or dime he receives. Another will put a twenty-five cent piece aside once a week. Any device of this kind is practical if the money eventually reaches the savings bank and is left on deposit long enough to give the force of compound interest a chance to act.

The man who began to put in a penny bank a five cent piece every day from the day his son was born could have benefited his heir and successor quite materially had he not grown weary of well-doing, and discontinued the practice. For five cents a day, earning four per cent compound interest, would have provided the young gentleman in question with no less than six hundred and six dollars and seventy-seven cents, on his twenty-first birthday; of which sum three hundred and eighty-three dollars and twenty-five cents would represent nickels actually deposited, and the balance, or two hundred and twenty-three dollars and fifty-two cents, would have been added *as the earning power of five cent pieces* while the boy was growing up.

Manifestly the difficult thing, the one huge strain on human nature, is not the money end of it, *but the Quality of Persistence.* A man who actually saves a five cent piece every day for twenty-one years has (without accounting for the leap years) put his hand in his pocket, drawn it out, and deposited the nickel in a tin bank seven thousand six hundred and sixty-five times. *That* is the test. We tire of it and stop; and the cost to us of stopping is the money we could have saved without any sacrifice, and did not.

This proves that the art of saving money,

involving regularity, patience, and self-denial is not only a money-maker but, far and beyond that, it is a character-builder. It results not only in giving a man some measure of independence in the end, but it makes him master of himself and of his affairs *all the way along.*

What savings accomplish in this particular for the individual, they do for a nation or a community. Chauncey M. Depew gave the following interesting illustration of this fact, in an address in the United States Senate:

I recall an instance in my own experience which illustrates the situation. In the village where I was born and which had many prosperous industries there never had been a savings bank. The artisans in the foundries earned good wages, but the shops were shut down during the winter and also when there was a depression in the trade. All of the workmen lived up to their wages, with the result that in these times of depression there was the greatest distress among them and their families. Thrift is not a natural gift, but an acquired habit. Self-indulgence is according to nature. An astonishing number of people must be placed upon their feet by agencies out of themselves, and kept there and kept moving by extraneous help. That accounts for the wonderful and increasing movement for the prohibition of the sale of liquor in the various states. All temperance laws were carried largely through the influence of the women. In one of the great conventions of the ladies of Georgia, one of the orators said:—

"The reason why we want and must have this legislation is that our men are temperamentally so constituted that they cannot resist temptation."

There settled among us in the early years of my practice at the bar a savings bank man from New York. He called together the citizens and organized an institution. As an example and to start it, all who could deposited a hundred dollars. The hundred which I put in, and which represented the extent of my capital, I have never touched to this day, though nearly fifty years have elapsed. Its influence as an anchorage in all crises of a long life has been incalculable. It required eight or ten years to cultivate among the people the saving habit, but when success was assured for the bank, distress disappeared among the artisans and workingmen of the town.

The money for the rainy day was in the savings bank and hard times were tided over without suffering, though a greater gain was that in these deposits were the beginnings of the purchase of homes. Before that time for an artisan or workingman to own his home was exceedingly rare, but afterwards it became the rule and not the exception. Good citizenship, a keen interest in public affairs, the prosperity of the church and the school, were all incalculably promoted by the independence and self-respect in the ownership of homes.

CHAPTER XIII

THE POSTAL SAVINGS BANK

All nations thrive when the government is a good banker.

It took forty years of agitation before the Postal Savings bill became a law on June 25, 1910.

As a result of this long delayed and bitterly fought act, millions of dollars have been deposited by the people of the United States with the government.

In an address before the American Bankers' Association, Theodore L. Weed, then director of the Postal Savings System, said:

On January 3, 1911, the Postmaster-General opened depositories experimentally at a single post office in each one of the forty-eight states and territories then existing in continental United States.

Within a year after the conclusion of four months' experiment with these offices twelve thousand additional depositories were designated, including the seven thousand five hundred post offices of the Presidential class. Additional offices will be selected at the rate of one thousand a month.

The receipts at six thousand of these depositories are being deposited in local banks which also receive the funds from the remaining seven thousand offices situated for the most part in small places where there either were no banks or none willing to qualify. The total amount to the credit of depositors of the System on September 1st is estimated at twenty-three million, two hundred thousand dollars. This sum stands to the credit of about two hundred and seventy thousand depositors, or an average of about eighty-five dollars for each account. The figures given do not include one million, three hundred and fourteen thousand, one hundred and forty dollars that have been converted by depositors into postal savings bonds.

It is needless to remark that the deposits are radically influenced by the restrictions contained in the Postal Savings Act limiting the amount that may be deposited by one person to one hundred dollars a month and restricting the total balance receivable from one depositor to five hundred dollars.

It has been already demonstrated that the amount of money which the Postal Savings System causes to be withdrawn from banks is a negligible quantity and that a very great proportion of the millions now on deposit represents money that would never have found its way into any bank.

Practically speaking, therefore, every dollar deposited by the Postal Savings System in the banks of the country is so much gain in deposits. This being true, it is clearly to the interest of the banking institutions to encourage and stimulate this new branch of the Federal Government.

The present limitation of deposits in the United States is much lower than in nearly all of the European countries, although the per capita wealth and average income here are much greater.

Many foreign countries place no limitation on the amount that may be deposited in the Postal Savings Bank; others, although having a limit on deposits, place it much higher than five hundred dollars.

In Italy, Holland, Belgium and Sweden and several other countries there is no limit on the amount that may be deposited, but it is provided that no interest shall be paid on the deposits in excess of a certain sum.

A writer in the *American Leader* (September, 1913), thus simply expresses the operations necessary for the depositor in the Postal Savings Bank to know:

The depositor merely fills out two duplicate certificates of deposit, one of which he keeps himself and the other he gives to the clerk of the postal bank. The postmaster of each branch of the system is held responsible for errors and submits a monthly account of his business to Washington, where it is verified by the inspectors who examine his accounts.

The certificates are engraved in even denominations, and a new depositor is supplied with a heavy manilla envelope on the outside of which are written his name, address, occupation, date of birth, parents' names, and other facts to identify him in case of necessity. The certificate is good only when presented by the person who fits the description and can write the same signature which the certificate bears on its face. It is thus as difficult for a thief to cash one as it is for him to dispose of a travelers' check. In the two years during which the Postal Savings System has been operated, there have not been more than half a dozen cases of forgery, and these were all due to the failure of the postmasters to take ordinary precautions in identifying the signatures.

The great advantage of this simple method of conducting the banks is that it requires only twelve bookkeepers to keep Uncle Sam's postal banks accounts, whereas, with the pass-book system, England requires two thousand bookkeepers and one thousand additional clerks. The world is beginning to study our system, and Japan is already considering its adoption.

The System has been popular with small depositors from the very start, and now, after only two years of operation, it is practically self-supporting. In fact, Postmaster-General Burleson has just added a "banking by mail" feature to the System, which practically brings the bank to the door of every man in the country. The System has found greatest favor among the foreign-born, who have more than half of the total deposits. And, while the international money orders sent abroad fell off twelve million dollars during the second year of the System's existence, the amount of postal deposits mounted from eleven million dollars (the first year) to twenty-eight million dollars, and there are many more millions hidden away in odd corners which will in time be brought out and put into circulation by being placed in one of Uncle Sam's banks.

Finally, the System is making of us a nation of savers. We are forming the habit which is probably the best habit of all—storing up against a rainy day without removing our hoardings from active circulation. It is a question whether France will continue to hold the record as a nation of small savers, if the amount of our postal savings deposits keeps bounding upward as it has been doing thus far. And the beauty of it all is that the regular banking institutions, far from being disturbed, are really benefited, in that more money is kept in circulation and the chances of national panic greatly lessened.

It is to be borne in mind that the figures given above are based upon the last fiscal report. The actual present postal deposits are estimated at over thirty-five million dollars.

Deposits in the Postal Savings Bank draw a low rate of interest, two per cent. Money may, however, be reinvested in government bonds.

At any time that your deposit is sufficient you can exchange your certificate of deposit in the Postal Savings Bank for Government bonds. These bonds bear two and one-half

per cent interest.   But the most interesting
feature about them is their denomination.
They are issued for amounts of twenty dollars, forty dollars, sixty dollars, eighty dollars, one hundred dollars, five hundred dollars,
and so on.

It is probably true that few people know
that they can buy a United States Government
bond for twenty dollars.   This makes it easy
to become a bondholder.   These bonds are the
best kind of security in the world.   They are
a positive asset and non-taxable.

By the purchase of these bonds freely by
our people, the art of saving should become
more widespread than it is.   The interest return is not high, but the security is worth the
difference, especially to those people who do
not know how to buy general market securities paying a higher interest rate.

If there is no Postal Savings Bank yet arranged at your post office, you may expect to
have one later.   In the meantime, ask for it.
Undoubtedly the Post Office Department will

make postal banks universal as soon as the demand is of like character.

Money hoarded under a brick in the fireplace or in an old stocking is withdrawn from circulation, and is practically useless. It has stagnated. Further, it brings no interest, and it may be lost or stolen. Such funds are far better brought out of hiding and put to work. Once you become the owner of a bond, even of twenty dollars, you will try to keep it in your possession; while twenty dollars in loose cash is easily parted with, because it is in cash.

Begin with a dime.

Keep it up until you have saved dimes enough to buy a bond.

Do not part with the bond.

Save the interest.

Keep on repeating the operation.

You will then be able to pension yourself.

And, all the while, your money is safe.

CHAPTER XIV

LIFE INSURANCE

Why spend for uncertainty, when protection can be bought?

What is Life Insurance?

In "Money and Investments," by Montgomery Rollins, it is thus defined:

"Life insurance is nothing more nor less than depositing one's money in a savings bank (that is, at savings bank rate of interest), to which is attached the gambling feature of the company that the insured will live beyond a certain period, and the policy holder accepting the wager, and betting that he will not."

But in the practical run of life, a life insurance policy stands for a good many things that are worth while.

For example:

You are married. A wife and children are dependent *upon what you earn every day.*

Suppose you earn fifteen dollars a week, or seven hundred and eighty dollars a year.

It would require fifteen thousand, six hundred dollars invested at five per cent to produce that income of seven hundred and eighty dollars.

Hence, as a working organization to your wife and family, you are worth fifteen thousand, six hundred dollars not to mention love and affection. Of this sum your health is a large asset.

Should you die without savings or life insurance, you can readily see in what position your loved ones would be.

This situation makes life insurance absolutely necessary.

As preliminary information, these facts are valuable:

Life insurance is a safe investment. All the standard companies are trustworthy and strictly honest.

The younger you are when you take out a policy, the cheaper the rate will be.

This means that for a small sum paid every

year, you buy more protection for your family than you would probably save in cash.

You must take a medical examination. If you pass, you have the great satisfaction of knowing that you are a good risk; of good health, with the average life expectation or better. Even this is worth money.

Then you take out your policy.

This requires regular payments, which make you a systematic handler of your money.

Being systematic will teach you to eliminate waste. Waste makes more people poor than anything else on earth.

A policy kept up to date will remove worry from your mind. You know there is something ahead for the family should you be taken away. This is a comfort you cannot imagine until you actually have it.

Great as the amount is of life insurance in force in the United States, it may be said, and well within the truth, that too many people have not availed themselves of this excellent means of family protection.

It is not the purpose of this text to recommend (1) companies, (2) forms of policy, or (3) amounts of policy, beyond this:

1. No one, however much the amount of insurance he proposes to carry, should hesitate to apply to the companies whose business, integrity, and resources are of the highest character.

2. The form of policy to be taken out is generally a matter of individual adjustment.

3. The amount of the policy is again to be determined by a man's earning capacity and all that conditions it.

It has not infrequently been reported in the newspapers that men of large means carry policies aggregating a million dollars or more. A more interesting news item which will be printed some day in the future, will relate that the standard companies have undertaken a general publicity campaign to educate the wage-earning class into the necessity of a far more wide-spread use of life insurance than is now made.

The working class, by which is meant, the mass of workers on moderate salary, have no claim in the statement that they cannot afford it. Thousands of men are deciding every day of the year to spend their money in favor of beer or tobacco as against life insurance and savings. It is poor comfort to a woman who has done her share of the family corporation work over a period of years to lose her husband and to find herself with nothing but the reflection that "there could have been a life insurance policy if we had only thought a little more about it." Even a few hundred dollars, in such an event, is a blessing.

Suppose a young man marries at the age of twenty-three, and for the protection of his wife and the children that may bless their union, let us suppose he can carry only a one thousand dollar policy. What financial sacrifice will it cost him?

This query addressed to an authority on life insurance brought forth the information that the best *form* of policy in this case is a Twenty payment life. This means that while the policy is payable only at death the payments are completed in twenty years.

Therefore, worked out theoretically, the young man would pay the annual premium, which at the age of twenty-three, is $29.10, up to and including his forty-second year. He will then own a paid-up policy (one on which no further payment is to be made).

But should he die before the twenty payments are made, his estate receives one thousand dollars. As a matter of fact, however (and should he live), he will find that by the accumulation of dividends on his policy his payments will cease, not at the twentieth year, but about the sixteenth year.

This is an approximation, but it is nearly correct and his total cost, should he live to complete the payments, would be as follows:

16 payments at $29.10........$ 465.60
Completed payments add to his

estate 1,000.00

But his estate has gained in value this $1,-000 the moment the first premium is paid. That is the essentially beneficial and practical side of life insurance.

Should a man attempt to add a house and

lot to his estate, valuing them at $1,000, and having the privilege to pay off the purchase at the rate of $29.10 per year, it would take him about thirty-four years to accomplish it.

Did he die before the payments were complete his estate would have no further claim in the property than the total of his payments. And it would be difficult to recover that if for no other reason than that property values are uncertain and property cannot be closed out at a moment's notice. But in the event of a man's death his life insurance policy is worth its total face value and no litigation is necessary to collect the money.

Here is a form of guaranteed protection without which no family dependent upon regular wages should fail to provide. To begin with, the day of death is uncertain; but a policy is certain even if a man should die five minutes after he takes it out.

While little has been done in an economic organization to protect and guarantee a wage earner's income, every possible device has been adopted to protect his life insurance policy.

Few men, whose limit is a one thousand dollar straight life policy, could ever save that amount of money as a future protection to the family.

Many a conscientious man worries about the future of his loved ones because he is not "getting ahead." For a small amount of money expended annually he could do two very desirable things, (1) he could remove the worry that always results in decreasing a man's working efficiency, and (2) he could actually protect them.

The man who has taken out a life insurance policy solely for the protection of his family should hesitate a long time before he allows himself to avail of his privilege to borrow upon it. When he looks the matter squarely in the face, it must be clear to him that he is not borrowing from the insurance company, *but from his wife and children* A protective policy reaches out not only to a man's money but to his honor.

CHAPTER XV

BONDS

The Bond must be as good as the Word.

Not until very recently has the attention of the public been called to bonds as an available means for the investment of small savings. Formerly, the majority of bonds were issued only in comparatively large denominations. Even issues as low as five hundred dollars were too large for the wage earner or the man of moderate salary. Of late, however, considerable attention has been paid by bankers and brokers to the needs of the small investor, and, in consequence, there is now a considerable choice of bonds in the denomination of one hundred dollars, and a few municipal and industrial bonds in still smaller denominations.

These bonds are being offered to a new

class of investors. They are people who never before purchased bonds, and whose savings were confined to the savings bank. A widespread campaign of education is being directed toward this class of investors, which undertakes to show why a hundred dollars is better invested in a good bond than left in the savings bank. Several points are emphasized in this educational propaganda that merit the attention of anyone who is able to save even small sums regularly.

It is pointed out that a bond pays interest from the day you purchase it. On the other hand, a savings bank often holds money several weeks before it admits it to interest earning.

A bond pays interest to its holder up to the day he sells it. But interest is credited to deposits in a savings bank only on specified dates, and if withdrawn wholly or in part before these dates, the interest is sacrificed.

By reason of fixed interest dates, the savings bank gets the use of considerable sums of money over a considerable time, and pays nothing for the privilege. In fact, the savings bank does not pay any return whatever on a large sum of money belonging to its depositor, but which it uses to earn money. But this peculiarity of savings bank interest is a matter of contract, clearly stated by the bank and subscribed to by the depositor.

In states in which the laws governing savings banks are strongest, the depositor is assured of the first qualification he must seek in an investment—safety. Now, a high degree of safety in any investment is always accompanied by a comparatively small interest return.

In the case of the bonds now being offered to the man of small means, it is pointed out that while the savings bank pays only three and a half to four per cent., bonds may be purchased that yield as high as six per cent. It is the temptation to secure a high interest rate that leads many people of small means into embarrassing situations that rarely come about through the savings bank.

The small investor must, if he prefers to

purchase bonds, acquaint himself with a few facts that will help him to keep clear of financial disaster. There are several classes of bonds—known as (a) First Mortgage, (b) Convertible, (c) Equipment, (d) Debentures, (e) Refunding, (f) Convertible Debentures, (g) Collateral, (h) Private Lien, etc. These, and several other terms descriptive of bond issues, are designations that specify the place of the bond in its claim against the property of the issuing company. First mortgage bonds, as the term implies, are a direct claim upon the whole, or a specified portion, of the issuing company's physical assets. Another form of bond, the general debenture, for example, carries absolutely no mortgage guarantee, and is generally issued against the credit of the company. Such bonds, are in reality, a form of preferred stock, the interest upon which is safe in good times, and no more certain than that of stock, in bad times.

It is essential for the small investor, in buying bonds of low denomination, to get a definite statement as to the kind of bond he is offered. If he does not know how to ascertain the status of a bond, he should inquire about it. Let him submit it to an officer of his savings bank, and to a business man of integrity who is in no way interested in the bond or in the company issuing it. While no bank can guarantee the future of a bond it sells to a customer, the bankers of the best class leave no stone unturned to be assured before they offer it that it is worthy of their handling. The best bankers take the most scrupulous care to offer only high class bonds. Hence, the small investor should make it a rule to buy no bond, even if it be only of fifty dollar denomination, of any but a bond dealer of the very best reputation.

The next rule is to prefer a first mortgage bond over any other. The bondholder is then part owner in the actual property of the company whose bond he has purchased. Next, he should prefer a listed to a non-listed bond. A listed bond is one recognized by one or more of the great stock exchanges of the world, and may be for that reason more readily disposed of.

It must be further remembered that no bond that combines a high degree of safety with ready convertibility (that is, ready sale) can pay a high rate of interest. A recently published bond list shows approximate annual yield from two and nine-tenths to six per cent. What are known as gilt edge bonds, pay little if any more than savings banks, but these securities may be bought at times at a price low enough to afford the purchaser the opportunity to sell at a high price. As a rule, however, bonds of the best type fluctuate in price only slightly.*

Having safeguarded his purchase, the small investor pays his money and receives his bond, generally with coupons attached, each coupon bearing the date and amount of interest due semi-annually. On the date specified, the owner cuts the coupon from the bond, and he may deposit it in a bank just as he deposits cash or a check; in fact, a coupon is a check

* See page 157, on interest return.

issued with the bond to the holder thereof in payment for the loan, and use, of his money.

But what can the average small investor do with a fifty or one hundred dollar bond? The moment he receives it, he feels that he owns something he cannot take proper care of. It is too valuable to be left in a closet or a bureau drawer; it cannot be carried in one's pocket, and unless kept in a safe place it may be lost or destroyed by fire.

The first thing to do for protection is to take the number of the bond so that it may be traced in case of loss. Generally, issuing companies will register a bond in the name of the owner. The best protection for it, and for all papers of permanent value, such as deeds, insurance policies, and the like, is a safety deposit box. A box may be rented for five dollars, or less, a year. They are provided for in banks and the offices of trust companies, and they are practically a guarantee of security, for a box has never been known to be opened by anyone but the owner.

Having now purchased a bond and provided it with a secure place of refuge, the bond holder has only to cut his coupons as they fall due. This simple act of cutting money from a piece of paper is apt to lead one to undervalue it. When it comes so easily one is tempted to spend it as easily. Make it a rule to deposit bond interest in the savings bank at once, and let it contribute its portion to the sum necessary to buy the next bond. In this way, adding interest to principal, there results a constant augmentation of the savings account, and the principal increases rapidly.

The small investor must remember that he may buy a bond, say of one hundred dollar denomination, either at par (one hundred dollars), or less than par, or above par, but if he holds it until maturity (the date when the principal is to be paid) he will receive par for it. Sometimes bonds are issued subject to call before maturity. This call feature is often at a price above par.

The small investor who makes the savings bank the depository of whatever small amounts he can set aside; who buys small denomination bonds with great care; who keeps his bonds in a safe place and never fails to deposit the coupons in the savings bank, will be surprised how rapidly his fortune will increase.

CHAPTER XVI

THE VALUE OF MONEY

It is the *love* of money that causes evil.

Money, being the equivalent of labor and its direct product, can be given in exchange by the earner in turn, either for labor he cannot himself perform, or for products he cannot produce. Thus, the man who is so skillful in making high grade cutlery that he can dispose of his production, receives money for it which he can in turn expend for the things he has no skill to make and produce. Hence, he buys a clock, a ton of coal, a brush, a hat and the like with his money. Apparently it is his money that permits him to make the purchases; strictly speaking, it is his cutlery-making knowledge. A producer, then, is one purveying the products of his craft to the world, receiving payment ultimately in exchange. What he makes he exchanges by way of swapping money for what he cannot make. It used to be the custom for the farmer to take his produce to market and swap it directly for what he needed and could not raise. The basis of value in money was not physically present in the transaction. We do the same thing to-day, only the money is often present in the operation.

In all purchases, then, a man exchanges his skill for something he needs and cannot make. This point is emphasized here, because the average spender of money entirely overlooks it. His earning capacity should be his standard of fixed values. When he has divided his week's income by the total number of hours it takes him to earn it, he knows what his time is worth. He must ascertain this by dividing the week's income by all the time included from leaving home to his return. Thus, on an over-all time expenditure of ten hours that bring him in four dollars, he must fix his value, not merely in the terms of forty cents an hour but in the statement that every forty cents spent is the present maximum power of his skill, time, thought and strength for sixty minutes. By substituting the latter statement for the former, he knows what things cost in the terms of the actual earning capacity.

Once he begins to set values on this basis, he will be more apt to extend justice to himself in all financial transactions. Assuming he is permitted to work from twenty to sixty on this basis of value, forty cents per hour, losing no time from idleness or illness, he will be able to draw his income for one hundred and twenty thousand hours. These one hundred and twenty thousand units at forty cents each will earn him a total of forty-eight thousand dollars. This apparently large amount of money must pay all necessary expenses for forty years, and build up that future protection for the possible years of decreased production after sixty. His income earning power increases from twenty and decreases from fifty, but his savings, if he sets them aside regularly, will increase. We may represent him as follows:

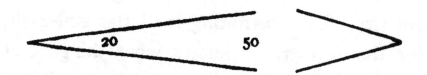

While we are assuming a uniform and continuous income in this case, there should be, as the diagram shows, an increase in earning power, reaching its height between forty and fifty.

Reverting to the cost of purchases on this basis of income, we now see that an expenditure of forty cents includes not only the value of a full hour of labor; a certain toll must be expended for every work hour to build up the future protection fund. This cost must be reckoned with in all money spending.

Let us further suppose, only for the sake of a definite illustration, that he so manage his affairs as to live on three of his four dollars per day, saving one. This means that ten cents of every forty is to be set aside for the permanent fund to be available at the age of sixty. At the beginning, in the first year, that is, when he is twenty, the ten cent piece he should set aside has an ultimate value at four per cent interest compounded annually, of forty-eight cents. The dollar he saves daily in that year will be worth four dollars and eighty cents, while the total three hundred dollars which he should put aside in the first work year will have increased to one thousand, four hundred and forty dollars.

The question, then, is this: Shall he, at twenty, dependent upon his own resources, and compelled to attain to a fund that shall protect him possibly from the age of sixty, waste a dollar that has a value to his own fund of nearly five times itself? Read in these terms: every five cent piece is twenty-five cents; every dime is fifty cents; every dollar is five dollars.

But a skillful and economic worker should, beginning at twenty, not have to continue for forty years at a level of income as instanced here. He should increase his earning capacity, and, consequently, his savings.

The illustration, however, is valuable in this: It shows that money is to be valued by the individual in terms *of what he has to do to earn it*. Further, it shows that taken over a considerable period of time, money has an enormous power to increase. This increase helps a man who works on a forty year plan, to establish a comparatively large fund from average wages. Even a man of forty-five who has never saved, but is, at last, convinced that he must do so, has a great time opportunity in a twenty year schedule. Every dollar he sets aside in the first year is worth approximately two dollars and twenty cents in the twentieth year. This means that every wasted dime is really twenty-two cents; every wasted half-dollar is one dollar and ten cents.

All earnings, then, are to be separated into three funds, and the value of every dollar's worth of labor (for labor produces the dollar) is to be determined in terms of the purpose of the fund.

1. The fund for immediate necessities. The value of the dollar of this fund is found,

first, by being sure as to what constitutes necessities—not confusing them with luxuries; second, by taking care to get the dollar's worth in every purchase. In a sense, money in this fund has no future value, or only a limited amount of it.

2. The fund for savings for future protection. Every dollar in this fund is valuable, not only as one hundred cents, but as many more as its increment will amount to at the end of the saving period. Ten years hence the dollar of to-day is worth one dollar and forty-eight cents; in twenty years, two dollars and nineteen cents; in thirty years, three dollars and twenty-four cents; in forty years, four dollars and eighty cents—and so on; these amounts being at four per cent compound interest.

3. The surplus fund. There may be now and then in hand some unexpended money after the two preceding accounts have been paid. There are several uses for this money:

a. Some of it should be set aside to make up a small cash emergency fund.

b. Or, it may be added to the regular savings account in anticipation of a day in the future when it may be hard to keep up payments to this fund.

c. Or, it may be spent after the manner described in Chapter XVIII, in philanthropy.

d. Or, it may, as the phrase goes, be blown in on luxuries and amusements. If it is, every member of the family should receive an equal share in what is purchased.

e. Or, it may be sanely divided between a, b, c and d.

The surplus fund left in hand after all these obligations are met, is the one that offers the most difficulty in handling properly. But, as we have seen, it may have many possible uses.

CHAPTER XVII

THE LIMITATIONS OF MONEY

There are millions of dollars on earth but not a penny ever leaves it.

It has been said, and truly, that no one needs much money for actual personal use. The amount any one of us requires for the necessities of life is small. But "necessities" for one man may seem like the most extravagant luxury to another.

Where shall the line be drawn?

That mirror of daily life, the newspaper, shows us that the line cannot be drawn. Here is a news item which states that Judge R. orders a man to pay fifteen dollars a week for the support of his wife and child. In the same issue of the paper, Mrs. B. petitions the court for permission to draw from an estate eighteen thousand dollars per annum, instead of twelve thousand, for the support and education of her daughter. The court grants the request. In both cases the amount is fixed at a sum deemed sufficient to provide the petitioner with the necessities of life. Apparently, then, the term is an exceedingly elastic one. In its lowest terms, it must provide shelter, food, and clothing. Beyond these, money can purchase countless things that may readily assume the phase of necessities after the manner of life to which the individual accustoms himself.

The world is full of things that create desires. It was recently reported that a society leader ordered several pairs of shoes to be made of the breasts of humming birds. It probably never occurred to this woman that there are thousands of people, especially children, who have no adequate protection for the feet; not enough to guard them against cold and dampness.

The well-to-do youth whose annual clothing outfit includes a dozen suits, is convinced, no doubt, that to have fewer would be a real hardship.

A man of fifty, who is a chronic borrower, owing money to every friend and stranger who listens to his tale, whose conversation turns to the high cost of living whenever anyone will listen to him, finds it necessary to be a member of six or eight clubs.

These cases, types of countless others, show that so far as the necessities of life are concerned, there is no limit to the variations that may be played upon the expression. There is no limit to the apparent need for money, once desire begins to lead the way. Two exceedingly serious social questions are included in the act of the woman who orders shoes made from humming birds' breasts:

1. Has she any moral right so to use her money in a world full of suffering and misery?

2. Is she not a benefactor to those working people who are skillful enough to make such shoes?

The money is released and goes into circulation. The woman gets the shoes, and several people receive payment for assisting in producing them. A distribution of money has been made that is beneficial. Whether it is the best possible distribution, is another question. But turning from the state of affairs that requires a woman and child to meet the demands of life on fifteen dollars a week, from the little girl whose up-bringing appears to the court to be reasonable at eighteen thousand dollars a year, from the countless children who pass through childhood shoeless and stockingless, and passing from the feet clad in humming bird shoes, we conclude that the necessities of life differ for practically every human being. But if we observe, even casually, the various types that make up our population, we discover that everyone, from the poverty-stricken to the over-rich, is subject to happiness and unhappiness; to content and to discontent; to joy and to sorrow. These conditions seem not to belong any more to the rich than to the poor.

Money is no guarantee of happiness, neither is the lack of it a necessary excuse for unhappiness. To be wealthy in material things does not necessarily imply equal wealth in mental and spiritual resources. It does not take long for rich or poor to learn that all the true pleasures of life are not to be had for money. If a man has learned to have joy awakened in him at the sight of a beautiful picture, it matters not what his condition is. The gift is his. The poor cannot sell it, nor can the rich buy it.

He who has found the way to enter into the delights of literature is rich, whether he possess much or little money. To be rich in the power of appreciation of beautiful things is a greater and a truer fortune than merely to have money to buy them.

It is not only art and literature that are free to all who have the power to understand, and possess without price in money; there are countless other things in life that are equally free to rich and poor. They are the things that build us up mentally and spiritually. Rich or poor, a man may be industrious, ambitious, and persevering. He may cultivate kindness, sympathy, and tolerance. With, or without, money, he may be to others helpful, lending a hand in the house of trouble, speaking words of comfort in times of grief and sorrow. Rich or poor, a man's mind and soul may go out to nature and be enlarged by it. Elihu Burritt never had the money to buy books in costly bindings or in rare editions, but he could read books in upwards of fifty different languages and dialects, and grasp the thoughts expressed in them.

Rembrandt, the painter, could not possibly have afforded at any time in his career to buy his own pictures at the prices they bring to-day; but he could paint them. Hugh Miller worked all his life in another man's granite quarry, shaping the stones that the owner might be enriched; but Hugh Miller, as a day laborer, learned to read the startling geological story of the earth as it is written in stones and fossils. Robert Burns received a few pounds profit on the first edition of his poems. To-day, a single copy of that edition costs a book collector two thousand dollars, or more. But

Burns had the heart and soul to write the poems, and the poorest boy and girl in the world to-day may read them, if they have the heart and soul.

That great fortune which lies in the true appreciation of the best things of life must be built by rich and poor alike if the joy of it is to be a solace. It is a poor man, a poverty-stricken man, who can pay thousands of dollars for the first edition of Milton's poems, but who cannot read Milton with delight.

This true wealth of life is free to all who want it. With it, the poor are rich; without it, the rich are in want. When the scholar earning two thousand dollars a year was offered an opportunity to earn fifteen thousand, his first question was: What will it cost me? His first impulse was to be sure what joys of life he would have to surrender for the additional twelve thousand dollars. And having determined that his time for study and investigation would have to be surrendered, that the greater amount of money meant fewer hours at home, he declined the offer. He was too rich in the essentials of his life to sell them out for money. Leisure, study, the attainment of culture, the joys of home and companionship are too often sold to the highest bidder, and, like Esau with his mess of pottage in his hand, we find that the eternal, spiritual birthright has gone in exchange for something we cannot take out of life with us.

In learning how truly to build a fortune, we must think upon the comparative values of permanent and transitory things. All the rarer pleasures of life may be had by rich and poor. They belong exclusively to neither class. But in making our fortune, we must never forget that there is much we cannot buy with money. For what we want we must not only pay the price in kind, but we must take the reward in kind. What we purchase through life, ultimately comes back to us, and once it comes, it is not to be shaken off. No man can work for money exclusively until the later years of life, and then find mind and spirit as rich as the pocket of his coat where the money is. All fortune, spiritual, mental, and material must be built daily from the beginning.

CHAPTER XVIII

LITTLE PHILANTHROPIES

Give and it shall be given unto you.

It is a question worthy of serious consideration, to what extent the beggar on the street is benefited by the money we give him. Does it help him onward, or does it thrust him deeper into the slough of dependence? This form of charity, if it may be so called, is undoubtedly more harmful than helpful. The advice of those interested in organized charity is invariably against indiscriminate giving. They hold that it tends to perpetuate a class of incompetent and dependent people that are better cared for by one or another philanthropic society.

We all make the acquaintance of the roving mendicant. He thrusts himself upon us, and we are at least obliged to hear his request

206

whether we help him or not. But we do not all make the acquaintance of the many philanthropic efforts that are directed upon those in need of help. In the great cities, especially, these organizations are many and efficient. An essential part of every man's training in citizenship lies in becoming intelligently acquainted with this factor of our social being.

We should give some attention to philanthropic efforts if for no other reasons than these: (1) They are a pronounced and effective factor in social life. (2) They take us out of ourselves and remind us that we are, after all, to an extent, our brother's keeper.

Every young man and woman intent on building a fortune, should determine to be, at the same time, a philanthropist. Whether we contribute time, active interest, or money, the effort is decidedly worth while, no less to the giver than to the recipient. Philanthropy is the gateway opening into a domain of human life through which all should enter. To do so deepens human interest and broadens human sympathy. It turns one's steps from the pursuit of purely selfish ends and directs them, when necessary, toward the relief of those in the abyss.

The crying need of the world is no less for human interest in the unfortunate than it is for money. Give a tithe of your time and thought and a tithe of your money, when you can, to the uplift and betterment of those who are in need. Direct personal interest in philanthropic activities is better by far than the uninquiring giving of a few dollars to get rid of the responsibility.

How shall you begin? You can readily learn the names of practical charities. Select any one that appeals to you. Secure information about it by inquiring. If it proves worthy of your interest and support, write to its officers, and through the reports and literature of the society learn the full scope of its activity and achievement. If, on thorough investigation, you are convinced that what you may contribute to it will result in the maximum of benefit to those whom it aims to assist, then adopt it as one of your interests in life. Do not judge its value to consist in what you do for it; take note of what it does for you. It is more than likely that you will agree after a while that you are the real beneficiary. Do not think of its cost to you in dollars, but of its benefit to you in a deeper understanding of life. You will find in a wisely conducted charity a source for much essential education; a phase of education, in fact, that you cannot afford to neglect.

We all have time and thought, even if we lack money. Men and women have been of indispensable assistance to others in exerting an influence for uplift. Clubs of boys and girls need practical and enthusiastic workers to inspire and to help. Many a boy and girl has been turned into the broad highway of opportunity by timely word or suggestion. You can contribute this, at least. The more earnestly you do contribute such help, the more you will think of practical ways and means of aiding the helpless. It will strengthen you, give you one more fixed purpose in life; it will prove to you that of all great things the helping hand is among the greatest. This interest will stimulate your thought, increase your power of organization, direct your effort to practical ends, and give you joy in worthy results accomplished.

Shall you give money, as well as time and thought? You should do so if you can. And you can, or not, according to your habits and resources, but chiefly according to your habits. It has been said that the Waste of the world could amply care for the Want of the world. Are you wasting what will supply what others are wanting?

Before determining, offhand, whether one wastes money, or not, it is worth while to stop for a moment to consider the great benefits that may be derived from small sums of money.

One cent per day may be spent for chewing gum, or saved in a penny bank for one year, will amount to a sum sufficient to give a child of the slums a trip to the country in summer. Or, it will purchase three or four weekly magazines for a year for a boys' or girls' club.

Five cents per day may be spent for a glass of beer or soda, or, accumulated daily for a year, it will provide winter shoes for several children, or a Christmas dinner for several families.

One ten cent cigar a day would clothe a college student, while fifteen cents daily would pay the entire tuition bill of a student in one of the smaller colleges for one year, with nearly five dollars over for incidentals.

Many of the most admirable charity organizations carry on their practical work, in large part, from annual fees of the members, of five dollars, or less than one and one-half cents per day. Five cents daily is almost sufficient to give you membership in four such organizations.

But never permit membership alone in charitable organizations to satisfy your philanthropic interests. The one valuable asset, alike to you and to the society, is direct personal interest. *Should you ever encounter a society that would rather have your money than your interest, give neither. A society that cannot discover a means of turning your interest to its own good is wrong somewhere.*

While some of the benefits resulting to you from an interest in philanthropy have been pointed out, there is another yet to be mentioned which is especially valuable. A genuine and unselfish interest in philanthropic movements is a character asset of the highest order. The young man or woman who is busily engaged in trying to win success, and who for no selfish purpose is also interested in the welfare of others, has thereby become a significant member of society. People of influence turn to such a person, willing to extend help and advice. And yet, valuable as this phase of the matter is, the greater benefit lies in the opportunity offered to develop through meeting and knowing the problems of other people and helping to solve them. This is a real investment in those things that bring satisfaction and content unto the end of life.

Careful inquiry into the Want of the world places the whole question of individual Waste clearly before us. One has a right to do what he will with his own so long as he keeps within the law. But whether one has the right to go through life, blind to the obvious misery about him, is another question, if one acts from the point of view of the moral law. Society may be wrongly organized; another order of things may, when established, banish poverty and disease; but, meanwhile, people hunger and suffer. Poverty crushes the ambition of the young. Disease mars the quality of citizenship for years to come.

While some are pondering on the great cure for these evils, let us not be oblivious of the fact that shelter, food, and clothing are as necessary now as they will be then. And let us determine individually, whether we are wasting what might be converted into the bare necessities of thousands, out of our portion.

While the investigation of charity through organizations is the simplest way to proceed, it is a question if one should not, at least, in part, organize his own charities.

In our own world of environment we come upon many an opportunity to offer the helping hand. The case before us may demand an immediate action or it may require consideration, but by inquiring we can generally justify the situation. The worst that has ever been said of organized charities is that they consume a large proportion of their total funds in working expenses. To give a dollar there must be two in hand. But this, while often true, is not always true.

Whether a man gives through organizations or through his own investigation, the essential fact for him is this:

Do not give as an easy penance, but out of a vital interest in people who, climbing the hill of life, bear a heavy load on a slippery path.

CHAPTER XIX

SECURITY FOR OLD AGE

Old? Who is old? You speak for yourself. I am ninety; full of youth and hope.

It has been pointed out that time is an indispensable factor in the process of money accumulation. Time permits money to increase, if it be left to work and to earn continuously. What is true of money and time, is likewise true of the effort that is stimulated by ambition. Increase of all kinds results from a continuation of the force natural in the thing. The little tree to become a larger tree must be left undisturbed to keep up its ceaseless round of activity in the quickening earth and air. Disturb it in either relationship, and the little tree will never increase, but disappear.

Ambition is like the little tree; the round of activity natural to it must never cease. Nor may it be said that it is ever full-grown. Where once a single stem and root branch made their way into air and earth, there is now a mass of growth advancing along scores of lines. We may no longer perceive it, but so long as the inherent force is at work, growth is going on.

The little tree must have time to become the big tree. So the incipient ambition must have time that its forces may establish their lines of action. Many writers have sung the praises of time, have urged the good use of it. But before one can use time to the best advantage, he must be inspired of something to pursue; he must have an ambition. It may be a simple ambition, or a lofty one, but it must be in him in some degree before he can make the hours of life render to him their tribute in some kind of increase.

Ambition being a person's fixed purpose to accomplish something and to be something, develops with the days and years as they come. There can be no day in the future of a true ambition when a man may say: "all is accomplished and I now stop." Ambition abides in the very life-blood of a man. When the force that impels it ceases, nothing but death can follow.

To the one intent on building a fortune, ambition will provide the way to travel. It is, at once, the direction and the inspiration. Ambition takes and retains the foremost place, and fortune-building follows after, as the result. The mottoes of Ambition are two:

I. A Way to go.

II. Something to be accomplished.

The virtue that resides in the "Way to go" does not consist in reaching places, but in enlargement through experiences that come to us as we proceed.

The "Something to be accomplished" is not to gain material things alone, but to become greater of mind and soul.

The incessant activity of the great writers and great artists is the expression of desire to BE more by doing more. All of them have worked after a single rule: Perceive clearly the thing to be done, then do it in the best possible way.

Some prominent men have apparently based their entire ambition on securing great wealth, casting all other considerations aside in order to become the possessors of more and more money. But it will often be found, among men of this kind, that ambition centers not in money itself, but in the activity that creates it. Money is, with many of them, literally a by-product. Such men are not fairly to be judged by the amount of money they possess, but by two other factors:

1. The nature of the activity that produces it.

2. Their use of money as it continues to accumulate.

Many wealthy men live lives of frugality; they are simple in their tastes and unostentatious in manner. It will always be found to be true with them that the essential interests in life are found in doing rather than in getting.

There are, likewise, many men of ambition

no less pronounced than these, whose entire round of activity scarcely touches money at any point. It is a negligible quantity even as a by-product. Something, however, impels them that is, in itself, worth doing.

It is in pursuing an activity worth doing that Ambition finds its highest expression. It depends upon the object pursued whether a man shall at the same time become wealthy. But, fortunately, wealth is a term that men interpret variously. What one man is willing to spend for a single picture, would be to another sufficient to give him life-long liberty to pursue scientific investigations for the good of all mankind. When Bernard Palissy was searching for the secret of the Italian glaze on pottery, he could not afford the time to earn money. Time itself was so valuable to him that he could not spend it for money. Yet, poverty-stricken as he was for years, the name of Palissy looms big in the history of achievement, to-day.

When Samuel Johnson in the days of hunger, wrote his great poem entitled Lon-

DON, he wrote with all the force of genius within him, and received ten pounds for his work. He never for a moment thought that what he spoke out of the depths of his misery would survive for a century, and after.

Ambition, then, does not always imply what we call financial success. If a man wants money, particularly if he wants much money, his ambition must include it, either directly or indirectly. The decision in this matter must rest in the man. Every ambition, whatsoever its name, must be justified in results. If one of the results is great material wealth, the use of that wealth must, in turn, be justified.

Recurring again to the little tree: it becomes a great tree only by fulfilling its natural impulse, as it can let that impulse work in its environment. The ambitious man may, unlike the tree, use his power of initiative to surround himself by conditions and environment that become more and more favorable to his development. This liberty to select and create carries with it the necessity to answer to the moral law which makes a man responsible for his acts in stewardship. By what process of thought and act did the helpless infant of sixty years ago become the powerful magnate of to-day? In that time, countless thoughts, intentions, and designs played to produce the result. The man of sixty is the lawful parent of them all. Is he proud of them? Then serenity will be his to the end. Does he fear some of them? Then he has hung a millstone about his neck that will grow heavier as he carries it.

A. Earning Power { Gross Income { Future Protection { Savings { Investments { Home, Securities }, Emergency Cash }, Life Insurance }, Current Expenses. }

B. Learning Power { Education { General Information gives Culture and furnishes, Special Training gives Skill and Efficiency and provides } }

Sum total of Estate
Home
Income
Cash
Protection
Mental resources for life.
Earning power into old age.

Chapter XX

WHAT CAN THE MAN OF FIFTY DO?

Whatever I have tried to do in my life, I have tried with all my heart to do well. What I have devoted myself to, I have devoted myself completely. Never to put my hand to anything on which I would not throw my whole self, and never to affect depreciation of my work, whatever it was, to find now to have been my golden rules.—Charles Dickens.

No one will deny that there are distinct advantages in beginning to save early in life. And for two reasons:

1. The habit, early established, grows in strength.

2. There is a longer period of distribution; and a larger portion of the ultimate capital is earned by the money itself.

This latter reason is well illustrated in this way: One dollar a year deposited in advance, at 4%, compound interest, from the age of twenty-five to sixty-five amounts to $98.82.

The same plan of deposit from thirty-five to sixty-five amounts to $58.32.

From forty-five to sixty-five it equals $30.96, and from fifty to sixty-five, $20.82.

Thus a young man or woman at twenty-five can accumulate nearly $10,000 by depositing $100 per year over a period of forty years. The actual amount of money deposited is $4,000, and the interest thereon is nearly $6,-000. (To be exact, $5,882.)

Therefore youth finds its advantage in time. But several conditions favor the older man. He is more settled in life; he has found himself; and others have found him; that is, they know his worth and reliability. There are (or should be) fewer temptations to draw him aside from a purpose. He is more capable of decision and of concentration. Much of the necessity of life is behind him. He has learned to work, has established his skill, and has chosen the few enjoyments he desires.

Beyond these apparent facts, he has worked up his earning power to a much higher level than it was in his early years. He has probably raised his family and feels that henceforth he can devote his energy to protecting the last years of his wife and himself. All these qualities and circumstances are in his favor. If it be that his health is good and his working capacity not perceptibly diminished, he has before him a score of years of possible activity. In itself, unimpaired health at fifty is a pension, for it means, in the natural order of things, years of fruitful activity.

If the man who has not saved much, but who has reached the age of fifty, bringing with him such qualities and the higher fortune we have described, he need not hesitate to begin. His health, skill, and mental attributes are all potent forces in his favor. Out of a moderate income the actual amount of money he sets aside may not be large, but he has so well conserved himself that it will be, in all human likelihood, ample.

It must not be forgotten, in planning to

protect old age, that a sound body, a clear mind and some capacity to take the world good-naturedly are as valuable assets as money; and they often pay far more satis-factory dividends. It has already been pointed out that if a man or woman has mental re-sources, being able to find pleasures in the better things of life, only a small amount of money is actually needed for individual ex-penses. An American scholar of small means lives in Oxford, England, pursues his read-ing and study, lives well as to the kind of room he occupies and the food provided him, for thirty shillings a week, or $7.50. And he is living in a degree of comfort far above what necessity would dictate.

An amazing number of men have married, raised a family and enjoyed neighborhood life on a few hundreds of dollars a year. In cases where health has been cared for they continue to live, as they have, to old age, and with no thought of retiring at sixty-five or at any other age. To the vast majority of men, no such thing as retirement from work can be considered.   And yet all men—did they realize it early enough in life—could by a little self-denial attain some degree of freedom.

The man of fifty has traversed the greater part of his journey.   Let him save what he can, but, above that in importance, he must have joy in life every day and, fortified by simple wants, find as much happiness as he can in the things of life and the thoughts of life that are incorruptible.

The art of building a fortune is not complete, does not express itself fully, if it fails to include mental treasures.   Let the door be kept ajar between the mind of the man and the cosmic mind of the Creator.   Then, with love and trust, one is spared a vast number of little trials that are vain expenses to those who have lived to themselves alone.

Many a human being has found happiness in life, and has given it freely to others, who never saw a bond and who could not describe a coupon.   Millions of people in the United States who are exempt from the Federal Income Tax will pass as happy, or probably happier, lives than those whose return to the Government is considerable. The king who wanted to buy the shirt of a perfectly happy man found the man, but he was shirtless. We must come again to the sage advice of the philosopher who said: Spend for power, not for pleasure.

Two things will keep any man in poverty, whatever his skill: Indolence and self-indulgence. Indolence does not produce. Self-indulgence does not provide. To reach middle life with no other call within us than that of a sensual appetite we are no longer capable of gratifying is to be poor indeed. Where self-indulgence has dulled the senses, ruined the digestion, weakened heart and lungs and nerves, what comfort is there in money?

He was skilled and far-seeing who advised men thus:

1. The way of success is to think and to work.

2. Never let work become so mechanical that it sinks to the common level. Lift it up.

Anything a man can do can be wonderfully done.

3. Take up the next task and do it with diligence.

4. Never expect to go forward from any point except from exactly where you are.

5. Avoid everything that depletes; and of all things that do this, fear is the worst.

6. Do not capitulate to any circumstance or condition. Fight as a soldier would, but never run away.

7. God speaks from many centers; listen to His messages.

8. Advance in wisdom daily.

9. The best basis for health is happiness.

10. The great rule is: Love one another, for by so doing love comes back to us a thousandfold.

Every man at some period in life thinks of these things; they may be dimly perceived or fully realized, but when they come to him the heavens open and the spirit of true living descends upon him.

We have all heard the expression: It would

be heaven to be rich. Heaven has been more discussed than any subject open to human kind. Simple philosophers, equally with the divine, have told us that it is a kingdom *within us*. Having once found it, a man may smile at compound interest, but let him sincerely believe that he can draw interest a thousand times compounded once he knows that the great Universal Mind is everywhere— within him and about him. And let him believe that at any age he can well afford not to save money, but he can never afford not to save and cherish that perception of life which tells him he is a god in disguise, capable of far more than has ever come forth from him. Not by might nor by power shall he make his way, but by the spirit. "A higher law than that of our will regulates events." To be rich in faith in that law is to be rich in reality.

CPSIA information can be obtained
at www.ICGtesting.com
Printed in the USA
BVHW011522090519
547856BV00009B/193/P

9 781095 729069